Thriving in Another Culture
A Handbook for Cross-Cultural Missions

Jo Anne Dennett

ACORN PRESS

Published by Acorn Press Ltd., A.C.N. 008 549 540 Melbourne
Office & Orders:
    PO Box 282
    Brunswick East
    3057 VIC
    Australia
    Tel/Fax for Australian orders: (03) 9387 2675
    Tel/Fax for International orders: 61 3 9387 2675

National Library of Australia
Cataloguing-in-Publication data
Dennett, Jo Anne, 1925- .
    Thriving in another culture: a handbook for cross-cultural missions.

Bibliography
ISBN 0 908284 27 6

    1. Intercultural communication. Missionaries. I. Title.
    266

Scripture references are taken from the Holy Bible,
New International Version, © 1973, 1978, by the
International Bible Society, used by permission of
Zondervan Bible Publishers, unless otherwise indicated.

Cover Design by Andrew Moody, Canterbury
DTP by Craig Longmuir, Lancefield
Printed by Robertson Printing, Notting Hill

Preface

The purpose of this book is to provide guidelines for Christians to live and serve effectively in another culture. Also, to offer means for sending churches and mission groups to become more effective in their task of fulfilling Christ's 'Great Commission' (Matthew 28:19,20).

God is stirring Christians around the world in a new way. Missionary movements are emerging in countries that once were missionary receiving regions. The churches in these countries are now sending their own missionaries to people of other cultures. 'More cross-cultural Protestant missionaries will be sent from, or within, the Two-Thirds World countries than from the West by the first decade of the twenty-first century.'[1]

However, there is often a lack of facilities for preparing and training missionary applicants in these countries. Many of the churches and emerging mission groups are not sufficiently experienced in selection and preparation of their applicants. This book aims to help meet these needs.

Regarding myself, I had wanted to be a missionary since age eleven, even though I did not know the Lord. Although I dreamt of becoming a doctor, my family was unable to afford such an education. My dream had to be fulfilled the hard way, by first undertaking nurses training and working as a nurse to pay expenses through university and medical school. I finally gained the Doctor of Medicine degree from University of Texas Medical School in 1955.

I became a Christian during my last year of medical school through the ministry of Inter-Varsity Christian Fellowship. After completing hospital practical training, I attended Columbia Bible College for one and a half years. That was a time of significant Christian growth, as well as training in sharing the gospel.

Eventually, Sudan Interior Mission accepted me for work

---

[1] *Mission Handbook* (1993), J.A. Siewert and J.A. Kenyon, Eds, Monrovia, CA: MARC, p.10.

among Muslims. I went to the Somali Republic in 1960 and served for twelve years as the only doctor in a hospital in a desert area. After a military revolution, missionaries were expelled from Somalia. Most of us went to Ethiopia where I served as medical officer at SIM headquarters, caring for missionaries and their children in the mission school.

A remarkable change came into my life at the end of 1973 — marriage to an Australian businessman, Bill Dennett. Adjustment to marriage and family life with two teenage sons was demanding. So too were the cultural changes of living in Australia. I battled with the loss of a missionary career which affected my sense of personal identity and worth. Through all these changes and stress the Lord's gracious care was demonstrated in many ways.

In Australia I have served on councils and candidate committees of mission agencies and I taught a missions course at a Bible College for ten years. My husband and I ran marriage seminars and Muslim evangelism seminars through the local churches. I undertook counselor training and ran a missionary debriefing and counseling program for ten years and now serve as medical coordinator for SIM.

Such diversity of training and life experiences provides me with unique credentials and a deep concern for care of missionaries in every aspect of their lives.

I hope the book will be a useful tool for short term workers and 'tent makers'. Many do not have adequate time to prepare and train for working in another culture. The information in the book can be used as a guide for missionaries on the field also when they face the issues discussed in the book. Questions at the end of each chapter will stimulate the reader to further thought and action.

I have tried to keep the style and form of writing simple, to use common words and short, clear sentences. A minimum of quotes and references to other publications is used. My aim is to accommodate readers to whom English is a second language and to make translation into other languages easier. This restricts the depth with which subjects can be addressed. For those who want more information, a 'Suggested Reading' list can be found at the end of the book.

I am convinced that biblical principles are relevant for Christian living and witnessing, whatever culture we come from, or go to. My prayer is that the principles advocated in this book will help missionaries to become effective communicators of the gospel and to live in a manner which glorifies the Lord Jesus. Also, I trust the guidelines for sending churches and mission groups will help their endeavors to spread the gospel throughout the world.

Jo Anne Dennett
Sydney, Australia

Contents

Introduction

Christ's Command and Christians' Obligation

God's compassionate longing is for all people to be reconciled to himself, that is, brought back from being an enemy to being a friend. His provision for this is through faith in Jesus Christ's death and resurrection as stated throughout the Scriptures.

The Bible must be the foundation for missions, not human ideas and strategy. We need the infallible word of God to equip and guide us in the extension of his kingdom. '*All scripture is inspired by God and is useful for teaching, for reproof, for correction, and for training in righteousness, so that everyone who belongs to God may be proficient, equipped for every good work*' (2 Timothy 3:16,17, NRSV).

When we come to know Jesus Christ as our Savior and Lord we want to proclaim the wonder of our salvation to others. God moves us to share the gospel with those who do not know of his redeeming love and grace. '*God has poured out his love into our hearts by the Holy Spirit, whom he has given us*' (Romans 5:5).

The main purpose of the church of Jesus Christ in the world today is to take the gospel to those who have never heard it. The channel through which this message is proclaimed is God's redeemed people. '*God reconciled us to himself through Christ and gave us the ministry of reconciliation... And he has committed to us the message of reconciliation. We are therefore Christ's ambassadors, as though God were making his appeal through us. We implore you on Christ's behalf: Be reconciled to God*' (2 Corinthians 5:18-20). What a high calling this is, to be ambassadors for Christ!

This Scripture gives a balance to the task of sharing the gospel in another culture. Much of missionaries' time is taken up with visitation, hospitality, material and physical care of people. These activities can be considered the **ministry** of reconciliation. Such contacts provide openings for sharing the gospel with people, the **message** of reconciliation.

Christ's commands to spread the gospel are to be obeyed.

Here are some Scripture references to consider, both commands and encouraging promises of his enabling.

Christ's commands to us:

- 'Therefore **go and make disciples** of all nations, **baptizing** them in the name of the Father and of the Son and of the Holy Spirit, and **teaching** them to obey everything I have commanded you' (Matthew 28:19,20).

- 'Repentance and forgiveness of sins **will be preached in his** (Christ's) name to all nations, beginning at Jerusalem' (Luke 24:47).

- '**You will be my witnesses** in Jerusalem, and in all Judea and Samaria, and to the ends of the earth' (Acts 1:8).

- 'But **seek first his kingdom and his righteousness,** and all these things will be given to you as well' (Matthew 6:33).

- '**Love the Lord your God** with all your heart and with all your soul and with all your mind' (Matthew 22:37).

- 'A new command I give you: **Love one another.** As I have loved you, so you must love one another' (John 13:34; 15:12).

Christ's promises to us:

- 'Then Jesus came to them and said, "**All authority** in heaven and on earth **has been given to me**"' (Matthew 28:18).

- 'And surely **I am with you always,** to the very end of the age' (Matthew 28:20).

- 'As the Father has sent me, I am sending you' (John 20:21).

- 'But **you will receive power** when the Holy Spirit comes on you' (Acts 1:8).

- 'And **I will do whatever you ask in my name,** so that the Son may bring glory to the Father. You may ask me for anything in my name, and I will do it' (John 14:13,14).

- 'And on this rock **I will build my church,** and the gates of Hades will not overcome it' (Matthew 16:18).

- 'See, **I am coming soon;** my reward is with me, to repay according to everyone's work' (Revelation 22:12, NRSV).

We should continually review and pray about these Scriptures to be sure our priorities in life and service are in harmony with God's purposes.

For further thought and action

1. What is God's longing and purpose for all people?

2. How does God accomplish his purpose?
   What is the channel he uses?

3. How do missionaries share the gospel?
   Is preaching the only means?

4. Is your vision for missions based on your own ideas or God's word?
   Explain your answer.

5. List some of Christ's commands regarding missions which we are to obey.

   Give Bible references for your answer.

6. List some of Christ's promises which enable us for the task.
   Give Bible references.

Part One

Living and Serving
Cross-Culturally

1

Preparing for Missionary Service

Case study: Paul is a Christian in a new missionary sending area. His letters illustrate questions and concerns which are common to such prospective missionaries. Read the letters, then think through the questions which follow.

To Dr J A Dennett

Dear Madam,

(I am not knowing how to write English. Please to forgive me. I write this letter in my language.)

I read an article you wrote in a mission magazine called 'Let My People Grow'.[1] A friend translated it for me. You wrote about helping missionaries grow from the beginning to the end of their careers. I am writing to ask you how to be a missionary.

I am just beginning and there are lots of things I need to know. My wife and I feel called to go as missionaries to a country which is foreign to us. We have prayed much about this and are excited about God's call for us to take the gospel to those people.

I have been a Christian three years and I read the Bible everyday. My wife, Maria, was raised in a Christian home and knows much more than me. She is a godly lady. We have two young children.

We have good Bible studies in our church. The pastor has trained us to share the gospel with people who do not know Christ. Also, how to help the ones who are converted to grow as Christians. But I know nothing about living and working in a foreign country. Could you tell me how to become a missionary?

Thanking you for your help,

Paul

(Please excuse me. I use my Bible name. You would find my real name hard to write.)

---

[1]The article mentioned in this letter is, 'Let My People Grow', by Dr Jo Anne Dennett, *Evangelical Missions Quarterly*, April, 1990, pp. 147-152.

Dear Paul,

It was good to get your letter. I was able to have it translated so don't apologize because you cannot write in English. I just wish I could write your language!

I am pleased to learn that you and your wife are thinking about missionary work. I hope I can be of help to you in your preparation for serving the Lord. You mentioned that you feel God has called you to such a ministry. It is vital for you to have that conviction but you also need confirmation of God's leading. Your feelings will fluctuate, so you should also have an objective basis for your commitment in order for it to endure.

I would like to suggest some steps for you to consider at this time. Here are some basic issues about which you need to consult your church.

● Do your pastor and church leaders agree that God is leading you this way and that you are suitable for such a ministry?

● Are they committed financially to helping you go overseas and to supporting you in a foreign land?

● Do you have a praying group of people behind you who will promise to uphold you and your family in prayer?

● Have you ever tried to share your faith with someone from another culture?

I suggest that you discuss these matters with the pastor and elders of your church. As you know from reading your Bible, Christians do not work alone. We are members of the body of Christ and must have other members supporting and encouraging us in whatever ministry the Lord may lead us.

I will be praying with you as you consider these matters and look forward to hearing from you again.

Yours in Christ,
Dr Dennett

Dear Dr Dennett,

I was excited to hear from you and ran to my friend's house to get the letter translated. He works in the American embassy and can read and write English real good. My wife and I read it many times and talked about it.

I showed your letter to our pastor and he thought about the questions you raised. He called the elders together to discuss your letter. After interviewing me and my wife they believe God is calling us to missionary work. They presented your letter to the church members and asked for their responses. As a result, a committee has been set up to arrange our finances and two godly ladies have organized a prayer group to pray for us. I feel really humbled over the way the church is encouraging us.

You asked if I have tried to share my faith with someone from another culture. We have a group of refugees from another country in our city. I went out to visit them and feel very sorry for them. They do not know how to read and speak our language, how to get a job, or buy things in the shops. They are so fearful and at a loss about everyday life in our country. Their children are totally confused in our schools. My wife and I visit them on Sunday afternoons and they are very happy to see us. They asked why we bother about them and I told them that it was the love of Jesus in our hearts. I hope we will be able to tell them about Jesus as we get to know them better.

We are the first members from our church to volunteer as missionaries and everything is new to all of us. You seem to understand our problems, so I want to ask you another question. Is there anything else we need to do or think about before we go overseas?

Your brother in Christ,

Paul

Dear Paul,

Praise the Lord that your pastor and church have responded so positively to your desire to become missionaries! Your going will enable the church to fulfill its role in spreading God's kingdom throughout the world. Since this is their first experience with sending out a missionary family you will need to keep them well informed of all your plans and activities. They need to be involved with you and to feel part of the team as they support and pray for you. They will be your 'life-line' when you are struggling in a foreign culture.

I was most interested to read about your concern for the refugees. Your description of their fears and confusion about life in your country is a picture of how you will probably feel when you enter a new culture. (A people's culture is their particular values, beliefs and customs expressed through their own language.) You and your family can identify with the needs of your refugee friends. You will have to struggle with a strange language, customs, schooling for your children, etc. when you enter another culture. I will be praying with you as you seek to share the gospel with these needy people.

You asked if there are other steps you need to take before going overseas. Yes, there are several things which you should do. God's word says, 'May your whole spirit, soul and body be kept blameless at the coming of our Lord Jesus Christ' (1 Thessalonians 5:23). This verse indicates areas of your life which require attention as you prepare for living and serving in another culture. In general, we relate to God with our spirits, to the world around us through our bodies and to other people by means of our souls. We need the Holy Spirit's control in all these aspects of our nature. They are not separate parts; each affects the others. 'A happy heart makes the face cheerful, but heartache crushes the spirit' (Proverbs 15:13).

Your **spiritual** state, and that of your family is very important. You may think you are doing well now but it will be different when you lack the teaching and fellowship of your church. You must learn to sustain a close, personal walk with the Lord in a hostile environment. When you take the gospel to people who are bound by non-Christian beliefs and practices, you will find that you are a target for Satan and all his demons. You must learn to use the weapons of spiritual warfare as described in Ephesians 6:10-18 in order to stand against the Devil.

Also, your **soul** needs preparation and nourishment. The dictionary defines the soul as 'the organ of emotion, mind and will'. We are constantly being influenced by the false values of the world. We need to be seeking the control of the Holy Spirit over what we think about, how we feel and react to upsets and the choices we make in daily life. The Apostle Paul advises us, 'Do not conform any longer to the pattern of this world, but be transformed by the renewing of your mind' (Romans 12:2). Daily study of God's word and prayer are the means of overcoming the pressures of the world, the flesh and the devil. These are vital matters for you and your wife to be dealing with now in order to be effective in your high calling as missionaries.

Your **physical health** is also very important. You should take your family to a trustworthy doctor and explain to him what you are planning to do. He will examine all the family members and take blood tests to make sure you are in good health. Also, he will advise you about the vaccine injections you require to protect you from the diseases which are prevalent in the country to which you are going. You may think this does not sound very 'spiritual' and that you can trust the Lord to take care of you and your family. But, remember, your body is the temple of the Holy Spirit and you are responsible to keep it working well. You cannot function properly if you or your family are frequently sick.

I hope this information gives you some practical ideas and steps to take in your preparation for overseas service.

Your friend in Christ,

Dr Dennett

Dear Dr Dennett,

Your letter gave us some things to do and think about. I am beginning to realize that being a missionary involves more than just getting in an airplane and flying to another country. In fact, I wonder if I am capable of being a missionary. I am not a great preacher or teacher. Do you think God can use an ordinary person like me?

Your friend,

Paul

Dear Paul,

I am sorry if my letter made you question your ability to become a missionary. You asked if God can use an ordinary person like you. The great teacher or preacher is honored and judged to be successful in the world's view. But we see in Scripture that God's ways are not our ways. He usually chooses to work through ordinary, humble people.

'Consider your own call, brothers and sisters: not many of you were wise by human standards, not many were powerful, not many were of noble birth... God chose what is weak in the world to shame the strong; God chose what is low and despised in the world ... so that no one might boast in the presence of God' (1 Corinthians 1:26-29, NRSV).

I suspect that no one feels capable of such a demanding task as sharing the gospel in a foreign culture. I certainly felt that way when I applied for missionary service. But feeling inadequate just made me turn more to the Lord. 'Not that we are competent in ourselves to claim anything for ourselves, but our competence comes from God'

(2 Corinthians 3:5).

We are conducting a Missionary Orientation Course here next month. I want to invite you and your wife to attend. You both would greatly benefit from the course. We would have an interpreter available for you. I am enclosing a brochure outlining subjects for discussion. Also, details about the cost, when and where the course is held.

Perhaps you should show it to your pastor so the church can consider helping you to attend. I think such a course is essential for every missionary applicant. One of the main benefits for you would be sharing with other people who are in the same situation as you in preparing for missionary service.

I have also enclosed some information for home churches and mission agencies which are now beginning to send missionaries cross-culturally. I trust this will be helpful to your pastor and church Missions committee as they get organized for sending you and Maria overseas.

Sincerely yours,
Dr Dennett

Dear Dr Dennett,

Thank you for sending the information about your missionary course. I'm sure it would be very helpful to us. I showed the brochure to our pastor and he consulted with the church leaders. They agreed it would be good for us to attend but the church is unable to raise the money at this time.

Could you write to me about some of those things you discuss in your course? It all sounds really useful and interesting. Do you have printed material you give to the people who attend your course? Could you send me copies? I still have a job and will pay for it.

I know you are very busy and must have many people like me writing to you. But we don't have any books about living and serving the Lord in another culture. I don't know where to find this information in my country. I think there must be many people like us who do not have such information available in their language. Maybe you should write a book!

Your friend,
Paul

Dear Paul,

Never apologize for wanting more knowledge! I am only too pleased to correspond with someone like you.

I am sending you by parcel post copies of the material we use in the Missionary Orientation course. I have tried to present the material in simple language and short sentences. I hope this will make it easier for your friend to translate.

I hope this information will be just the beginning of your thinking about these subjects. There must be a Missionary Training Institute in your region conducted in your language. I will find out where there is one near you and let you know. You will need to inform your pastor and church about the program and the cost for your family's training. I trust they will see the benefit of such training to equip you for effective service.

Please keep in touch by letter and feel free to share your thoughts and questions. That is how we all learn. I will be praying for you and Maria in all your preparations for missionary service.

Love and prayer in Christ,
Dr Dennett

P.S. Thanks for prompting me about writing a book on these subjects! I have been working on a manuscript and I will send you a copy when it is published. Then, you will have the job of getting it translated!

Questions on the case study

Think about your experience relative to Paul's in preparing for missionary service.

1. How did God call you to be a missionary?
   How did he make his will in this matter known to you?

2. Did your pastor and church leaders confirm your calling to be of God?

3. What prayer and financial support can you rely on?
   Is it adequate to sustain you in mission work?

4. How can you keep your home church informed so that they understand your plans and needs?

5. Do you have a regular time of Bible study and prayer?
   Is your fellowship with the Lord strong enough to sustain you when separated from your church and Christian friends?

6. How do you rate your physical, mental and emotional condition?
   Are you healthy and stable enough to cope in another culture?

7. Has your training been adequate to equip you for missionary service?
   What plans do you need to make for further study?[2]

---

[2]Assessment, interviewing and selecting of missionary applicants are discussed in Part Two of the book.

2

Realities of Missionary Life

Paul hopes to serve in another culture.
What awaits him there?

When new missionaries enter a foreign culture they go through a process not unlike a birth. Both processes involve drastic changes in environment and life support. The baby has been protected and nourished in the mother's womb during its formative months. Then, it is delivered into a cold, unfamiliar world. The cord is cut, severing the baby's life-line from the mother. The baby has to be stimulated to take its first breath of air. Its heart and lungs must take over the life-giving function the mother provided. The baby is helpless and dependent in its new, unfamiliar environment. It will be a few years before the baby can function on its own.

In a similar manner, missionary candidates have enjoyed the care and encouragement of their church and Christian friends. During the training period they probably felt secure and nurtured. They coped well in their own familiar environment. Then, the supportive links of family, friends and church are severed as they go into a new culture. They leave the comfort of their customary surroundings. They become like helpless babies, unable to talk and express their needs. They have to acquire new skills in language and how to relate to people in order to survive.

When we go as missionaries to another culture we experience exceptional pressures, in addition to those common to all Christians. Many people view missionaries as 'super saints', living above the struggles of other Christians. That is a false concept, failing to take into account the super stress under which missionaries live by the very nature of their calling. Even though they are strongly committed and motivated, they still *have this treasure in jars of clay* (2 Corinthians 4:7). They are subject to the same pressures on emotions, mind, body and spirit, as are others.

Special stresses

What are some of the special stresses of missionary life that make new missionaries so vulnerable? (We will consider how to handle these pressures later in the book.)

A study by World Evangelical Fellowship found that missionaries from some nations reported particular problems. For example, Koreans found inadequate educational facilities for their children a problem. Filipinos battled with inadequate financial support. Brazilians stated unrealistic expectations and inadequate theological training as major problems for them. These are particular national problems.

There are also problems common to missionaries from all countries which we will now discuss.

A new culture Moving into a new community, culture, language, job and life-style involves a tremendous amount of change. We leave the familiar ways of doing things and are thrown into a totally foreign environment. We are usually confused and frustrated. We feel like children again as we struggle to learn the language, customs and cultural clues in this new environment. Changes in our lives, both good and bad, cause much stress.

Spiritual warfare is another source of stress. Satan enslaves people who are without Christ and also attacks and resists the messengers of the gospel. This relentless battle affects missionaries spiritually, mentally, physically and emotionally. Spiritual dryness can easily overtake missionaries because they are often much too busy. The pressing needs of people in areas where there are so few Christian workers can cause missionaries to neglect their devotions and Bible study.

The lack of **personal support** which missionaries enjoy in their homeland is a major hardship. They miss the fellowship, the familiar customs and social activities to which they are accustomed. There may not be anyone around to understand their inner battles and to assure them of their unconditional worth in the Lord's sight. To have their values and beliefs constantly denied by others is demoralizing.

This means their sense of **self worth** is under constant attack. The national people may view them as 'stupid foreigners' because they do not understand the language and customs. Being continually denigrated can soon make people feel useless. This type of pressure causes missionaries to become discouraged and to feel they are worthless. Ethnic features, the color of skin, shape of eyes, etc. make the missionaries look different to the people·they serve. Nationals may ridicule anyone different believing that their type of features are best, since anything unfamiliar is suspect. (This factor may work to the advantage of some missionaries. For example, Latin Americans are very acceptable in North Africa because of their similar coloring and cultural background.)

Misunderstanding of **motives** is a heartache for missionaries. People may think they are in the country for personal gain. For example, our medical ministry in a developing country was heavily subsidized by Christians at home. We charged a nominal fee of three shillings (50 cents U.S.) per day for hospitalization and treatment. But the people used to say, 'You're just here to make money'. To single women they said, 'You must have come here to find a husband'. Muslims usually think missionaries perform good works to gain merit with God.

Expecting too much Missionaries often strive toward unobtainable goals because of their own or others' expectations. Constantly feeling a failure is very discouraging. This is a particular danger for those who feel they must do everything perfectly. For example, missionaries are unwise to expect to learn the new language in one year. Unless they accept their limitations they will break down.

Also, missionaries may have impractical expectations of others. They will have made tremendous sacrifices to live in another country but the local people there will have no way of knowing all that was involved. If the missionaries expect them to understand their sacrifices or be grateful for their services, they will be terribly disillusioned and disappointed.

Inter-personal conflicts Approximately 50 per cent of missionaries leave the field because of difficulty in working with some of their colleagues. Most missionaries suffer the painful tension of such conflicts at some time in their service.

Differences in nationalities, personalities, doctrine, style of ministry and the like, contribute to the problem.

Missionaries expect the national people to be different and are more prepared to make allowances for those differences than for differences with co-workers. However, there will still be misunderstandings with nationals and these can also cause much confusion and stress.

Pressures on **family life** are intensified. Missionaries' marriage relationships will be threatened because of the many demands upon their time and energy. If the husband is happily involved in church work but his wife is confined to home duties she will feel a lack of spiritual ministry. Also, conflict can arise from concern for their children's care and education. The family may be separated for several days each week if the wife and children remain in a large center for schooling while the husband ministers alone in an isolated area. Their children's welfare is a major responsibility before the Lord. However, the wife may feel guilty about spending more time with the children than in 'the work'.

Financial matters are of great concern for most missionaries especially if their home church is unable or unwilling to support them adequately. They may have to adopt a simpler life-style than the one they enjoyed at home. (This is more of a problem for those from developed rather than less developed nations.) For those who have been independent previously, it is not easy to become financially dependent on others. Missionaries need to see themselves as part of a wider team: they go while others support them by praying and giving.

When missionaries return to their homeland they often suffer **reverse culture shock**. Coming back into their original culture may be as traumatic as going to the field because this shock is unexpected. Missionaries face all the changes that have taken place in their homeland in their absence. They will have adapted their own life-style to that of the host culture and when they return they find that life in their home culture is drastically different. Missionaries and their children are happy to be with family and friends again but they also are sad because they miss the work and friendships they enjoyed on the field. They need to be prepared for the mixed emotions they experience at such times.

If we feel overwhelmed with all these problems, we must remember that Christians grow through challenges and trials. There is no greater opportunity for personal growth than to be a missionary. We prove the Lord's sufficiency for our every need in ways we never could in our homeland. There is no greater privilege than taking the good news about Jesus Christ to those who have never heard it. In the name of Christ we shed the light of the gospel into dark, hopeless lives. The gospel shows them the way of forgiveness of sin and peace with God, and offers them freedom from bondage to Satan and his demons. It brings sight to the spiritually blind and guides them into eternal life. To be missionaries is an enriching experience for all the family. It requires some sacrifices but is extremely rewarding.

Surviving the Pressures

So in view of all the pressures discussed above, what qualities do missionaries need in order to survive and thrive? Spiritual maturity is the major quality needed. Because of its importance a whole chapter is devoted to the topic (see Chapter 5). In general terms, missionaries need to be able to adapt, to endure, to walk humbly, to relate well, and to be sensitive within another culture.

Missionaries must therefore learn to be:

● **Teachable** To be effective in a different culture means becoming a humble learner in every aspect of life. If we think we are the great preacher or teacher who has come to impart all wisdom to the national people we will fail in our primary objective of sharing the gospel. The most profound example of a humble servant is demonstrated by the Lord Jesus in John 13. *'Jesus knew that the Father had put all things under his power, and that he had come from God and was returning to God; so ... he wrapped a towel around his waist. After that, he poured water into a basin and began to wash his disciples' feet, drying them with the towel that was wrapped around him'* (John 13:3-5).

● **Adaptable** to other ways of thinking and doing things. Things may be done differently but that does not mean they are necessarily wrong — just different. We must be flexible and learn to acknowledge this. In order to have an impact upon the people a missionary must adopt what is good and helpful in the local culture. If we come from a work and time oriented society, we will need to change our attitude to one where people and events are the main priorities. The Apostle Paul is an excellent example of adaptability. *'I have become all things to all people, that I might by all means save some'* (1 Corinthians 9:22, NRSV).

Missionaries must also adapt to the authority of national and local governments. We are guests in their country and should give them respect. This is not easy when an official is incompetent or tries to obstruct our Christian witness. Nevertheless, their position must be respected. *'For the Lord's sake accept the authority of every human institution'* (1 Peter 2:13, NRSV).

How we handle **disagreements** is crucial. In some cultures the acceptable way is to confront the other person and seek settlement of the issue. Other cultures practise the use of an intermediary who meets with the two parties seeking reconciliation of their differences. We must adopt the host culture's way of resolving disagreements and differences. Otherwise, there will be many unresolved conflicts to hinder our work and witness.

● **Accepting and tolerant** toward colleagues. This is fundamental. Most missionaries expect to make adjustments in regard to the nationals, who will obviously have different customs and practices. But they may fail to realize there could also be major differences among their fellow workers. Thrown into the company of colleagues with various personalities, nationalities and doctrinal differences, they may be little prepared for this area of great testing. In order to be willing to accept others they will need to develop a scriptural attitude to this matter: *'Accept one another then, just as Christ accepted you, in order to bring praise to God'* (Romans 15:7).

● **Available to God** for his purposes in our daily lives. It is vital that the Lord has first place in our priorities. Next must come our ministry to people and last our own work agenda. There is no 'time out' in effective missionary service. We may have a break from daily demands on a day off, but that does not mean we are free from our accountability to the Lord. We must develop a heart attitude which says, 'Here I am, Lord. I would like to catch up with my desk work but help me to welcome anyone in need who may come my way today.' That is easy for me to write but I failed in this area many times in a busy medical ministry in a developing country.

● **Dependable** This is becoming a rare characteristic in today's world but Christians should be people *'who stand by their oath even to their hurt'* (Psalm 15:4, NRSV). Those who are dependable and self-disciplined will be much more effective working in another culture than those who do what they like, when they like. Accountability is part of being dependable. Besides being answerable to God, missionaries need to develop an attitude of accountability to both their ministry team and their home church and supporters.

● **Persevering** when things are difficult, dull, or seemingly unproductive. Many new missionaries start in a blaze of glory only to quickly fade away like a shooting star. Paul's advice is, *'Therefore, my beloved, be steadfast, immovable, always excelling in the work of the Lord, because you know that in the Lord your labor is not in vain'* (1 Corinthians 15:58, NRSV).

● **Practical skills** are required for daily living in some developing countries. Basic skills worth cultivating are: cooking, sewing, hair-cutting, growing vegetables, use of computer, typing, book keeping, teaching, basic nursing and first aid, building, construction of wells and latrines, driving and motor mechanic skills.

Arrival on the Field

'I did not know it was going to be like this!' Most new missionaries utter this in their early days on the field. In spite of all the preparation, no one can imagine what life will be like until they arrive in the new place. Also, no one can predict their reactions to all the changes in their lives.

Many missionaries find their expected role on the field is quite different from their actual job. The field situation may well have changed since their original job description and they may be asked to do a different type of work to what was planned. This will challenge their flexibility and willingness to work as a member of a team.

When I went to the field I was expecting to run a hospital. But when I arrived, I found that the hospital was nothing but four walls with grass growing in the middle! I had to reassess my purpose in going to the field. Was I there to build a medical work or to build the church of Christ? I renewed my commitment to establishing the church. Then, I was able to press on with the job of running a clinic in our house, and then building and equipping the hospital, with evangelism being my main drive.

After arriving in a new culture, we need to slow down and give ourselves plenty of time to adjust. Our natural tendency is to begin 'the work' immediately, whatever it may be. But spending the first months in language and culture learning is both essential and beneficial. It may seem like lost time but will prove very productive in the long term. As a doctor I found it frustrating to be out of medical practice for six months. But later I was grateful for that intensive language study and cultural orientation period.

Wherever possible, you should have a senior person who can care for and guide you through the early adjustment period. You must be willing to listen, ask questions and learn. If you are new, it is wise to refrain from offering suggestions requiring change for at least a year. Then you will be more likely to understand how and why things are done as they are.

A new missionary arrived in a Muslim country zealous to make converts. He used Western methods of evangelism and wanted to baptize all who said they believed. The senior missionary counseled him that it was wise to have new converts grounded in Scripture first because Baptism is seen by the Muslim community as the final step away from Islam. That step inevitably brings opposition and persecution to new Christians. The young missionary thought this method showed lack of trust in the Holy Spirit and refused to change his ideas. He went his own way, unwilling to submit to his experienced elders. Needless to say, this resulted in division in the team and confusion for the believers. If he had only been willing to consider the senior missionary's advice, he would have been more effective and less disruptive to others in his ministry.

Some positive attitudes and actions that new missionaries should adopt toward their seniors are to:

- be patient with the situation
- respect the senior's position
- offer constructive suggestions sensitively
- acknowledge their own limitations
- be considerate of weary elders.

Serving within a framework

Personalities and styles of ministry of missionaries vary. Some people work best in a group and need the personal support of colleagues. Others are more self-sufficient and can function alone without being prodded. Fellow workers need to take this into account and not force everyone into the same mold.

A **team ministry** is usually more effective than one with individuals working alone. Senior missionaries can shepherd new ones. Christians have different gifts and a team can make use of the various gifts of the members. When a couple work in a team the contribution of both husband and wife should be taken into account, not just the husband's role.

The strengths and weaknesses of members of a team can also be used to advantage. For example, one person may be good at organizing but weak in personal witnessing. Another member may be excellent in evangelism but hopeless at organizing anything. The team members must be willing to delegate various aspects of the ministry to those gifted in different areas.

Belonging to a **mission agency** has many advantages. Agencies are able to arrange for language learning and orientation to the particular ministry of each missionary. Also, they have experience in dealing with national governments, obtaining visas and work permits, arranging transport within the country and purchasing supplies for missionaries in isolated areas. They are organized for providing medical and dental care for their members and schooling for the missionaries' children. New missionaries not associated with a mission group have to make their own arrangements for all the official and practical matters mentioned above. This is very stressful and time consuming for anyone new to the country.

Tent makers Some countries do not allow missionary activity as such and will not grant visas to missionaries. However, 'tent makers' can gain entrance by means of their jobs, professions and relief work. This type of worker takes its name from the example of the Apostle Paul. He used his skills as a maker of tents to support himself while he evangelized and planted churches (see Acts 18:3). Tent makers need special ministry skills, such as the ability to evangelize and disciple discreetly, to have a servant heart and to form genuine friendships. They need fellowship and nurture on the field through a local church and/or mission agency. They must be spiritually and emotionally mature and able to balance time between job and ministry.

Tent makers face special problems regarding their identity and security in the community. The national people and government officials may be suspicious of them. They will question the tent maker's motives for being in the country. 'Why are you working here? Couldn't you get a job in your country?' 'What are you talking about to those people who come to your house at night?' Also, the home church and supporters need to be aware of the risky position of the tent maker and careful in what they mention in letters.

In whatever type of ministry we are involved, we should keep in mind the need of the **whole person**. It is unscriptural to preach to people without concern for their material needs. Missionaries are needed for work among the urban poor, refugees, victims of famine and war, victims of AIDS and their families. Because these people are especially vulnerable they need the love of Christ to be demonstrated to them by deed and word.

For further thought and action

1. Do you think missionaries should be expected to live free of everyday problems? Explain your answer.

2. What stresses of missionary life do you foresee as particular problems for you? For family members?

3. What qualities do you need to develop in order to survive the pressures in another culture?

4. What personal strengths would you bring to a ministry team?

5. What personal weaknesses might hinder your team work?

6. List some advantages of working with a mission agency in a new culture.

3

Adapting to Another Culture

A Case of Wrong Attitudes

A young missionary couple, John and Sarah, finally arrived in their new land. Their major task was to learn the language of the people. They diligently studied the grammar book and practised the new vocabulary together. But when they went out among the people and tried to converse with them they felt uncomfortable. It was unpleasant being laughed at and ridiculed when mistakes were made. They felt like children again, just learning to talk. The people did not seem to appreciate that they were well educated with diplomas in their vocations.

They found it less stressful to study within the security of their own home and so avoid the discomfort of going out among the people. Sarah asked John to go to the market to buy food as it was easier for a man to bargain with the merchants. She would rather stay home to care for their baby. Sarah hated taking him outside where the people poked at the child and spat on him as a blessing. She certainly did not want a national woman caring for her baby. Who knows what the 'nanny' might feed him or do to him!

Gradually, John and Sarah found themselves more and more isolated. An attitude of fear and hostility toward the people dominated their thinking. They spoke of the people in a derogatory manner as 'those M's', not even using their full name. After cutting themselves off from the people they no longer had any Christian witness. They then convinced themselves that God had not called them to be missionaries after all and returned to their homeland.

This couple's story illustrates the wrong way to enter into another culture. They developed attitudes of superiority and prejudice which led to rejection of the people. They excused themselves and blamed their failures on the people. This inevitably resulted in feelings of alienation and hostility toward the people and the loss of their calling to missionary work.

What positive attitudes should John and Sarah have adopted in their new culture? Their adjustment could have been helped if they had accepted the people even though they were different. We can accept people as they are without necessarily approving of their behavior. This couple could have learned from the national people and observed how things were done in that society. Then, John and Sarah would have built friendships with the people and developed appreciation for their views and customs.

Some mission groups advocate the immediate immersion of new missionaries into the culture. They are placed in a national's home, or near vicinity, and eat, sleep and communicate only with nationals. The atmosphere certainly is conducive to learning the language and customs! The aim is to encourage **bonding** with the nationals and to prevent the formation of a 'missionary ghetto' mentality. The concept works best where there is an established church. It fosters a sense of responsibility in the church members to care for the new missionaries who have come to work with them. For some missionaries, such a program is overwhelming and causes harmful stress overload. A more gradual approach to the culture may be required.

All of us are born into a particular culture. Our views and values are molded by it. We are racially proud, and think our way is superior to all others. As Christians we need to re-assess the absolute values of the gospel and determine which of our views are cultural prejudices. As we identify some of these, we must be willing to shed ideas and customs that are not biblical, even though they are ingrained in our life style. Then, we can become immersed in another culture without constantly thinking, 'That's not the way we do it back home'. Our view should become, 'Their way is different, not wrong'.

Some Christians mistakenly think they are not affected by culture. They say their only concern is to preach the gospel, that their citizenship is in heaven. But we are still in the world and part of the human race. We need the structures of society in order to function. Christ came and lived among us as a human being except for sin. His citizenship is truly in heaven but he identified with us in order to make God's grace known to us. Therefore, we should enter into people's culture so we can make the gospel relevant to them. We must not think we are so spiritual that we can ignore people's customs and values.

No matter how clever missionaries may have been in their own culture, they must enter into another culture as learners. They should reject any sense of superiority or thinking they have greater knowledge. Even the Apostle Paul acknowledged that he did not have all the answers. *'Now we see but a poor reflection as in a mirror; then we shall see face to face. Now I know in part; then I shall know fully, even as I am fully known'* (1 Corinthians 13:12).

What is culture?

'Culture is an integrated system of beliefs, of values, of customs, and of institutions which express these beliefs, values and customs, which binds a society together and gives it a sense of identity, dignity, security and continuity.'[1]

When we look into a culture, we see it is made up of several layers. Observing it from outside, the more superficial layer is **behavior** (customs). This involves how the people do things, for example, they eat with their fingers.

As we go deeper, we learn some of their **values.** That is, what they think is good and right, for example, separation of the sexes in social life.

Beliefs are an even deeper layer and indicate what is true and what is false, for example, belief in many gods.

The **worldview** of the people is at the heart of a culture. What is real to them? For some groups the presence of ancestors' spirits is very real. The living must give attention and honor to them. Materialism is the heart of the worldview of Western and secularized urban groups. Reality for these consists of physical aspects of life, for example, food, housing, material gain.

Differences in cultures consist of many things. Some examples of what is important in one culture, compared to another are:

---

[1] From 'The Willowbank Report of The Lausanne Committee for World Evangelization', 1978.

Culture A	Culture B
● individual, independence valued	● group oriented, family honor valued
● time/work oriented	● people/events oriented
● criticism seen as honesty	● criticism brings shame
● direct settling of differences	● indirect, use of mediator
● equality, consensus decisions	● authority, patriarchal decisions
● value zeal of youth	● value wisdom of elders
● progress in technology best	● traditional ways are best
● materialism, value possessions	● spirit world, value blessing of the spirits

Cultural practices

New missionaries must learn and practise the cultural clues of their host culture. The following are some examples.

● Greetings are prolonged and extensive in many cultures. Just a quick 'hello' is unacceptable. The polite way is to inquire into the health and welfare of the person or persons you are greeting and of each of their family members. I found this difficult in medical work. My tendency was to say, 'Hello, how can I help you?' That was considered rude. I was expected to go through all the greetings, then as an afterthought ask why the person had come to the clinic.

● Who are you allowed to be friendly with in this society and from whom do you keep a respectful distance? Do you stand or sit in the presence of others, especially the elders and chief?

● Which group is inaccessible to you? In Muslim countries males are not allowed to associate with women outside their family group. Also, women are expected to dress modestly and avoid eye contact with men other than family.

● 'Body language' is very important in many cultures. For example, Latin Americans are warm, friendly people and stand close to the person with whom they are conversing. The English are very reserved and prefer to converse from a distance. Other body language clues are facial expressions, bowing, tone of voice, hand gestures, etc.

● Showing anger is offensive to some people and they are quick to discern signs of emotion. A national worker in our clinic told me, 'When you are angry your neck turns red; the nurse's eyelid twitches'. And we thought we were keeping outwardly calm!

● The manner in which food is eaten will differ. In some cultures you show your enjoyment by slurping and burping and scraping the plate clean. In other societies it is polite to eat quietly and to leave food on the plate to show they have fed you sufficiently.

Consider some of the important issues in your own culture and compare them to those of the new culture. This will help you to see where and what changes are necessary for you to fit into the new culture. Our activities and relationships should be determined by what is proper for the culture in which we live. Culture and Christian values will be discussed in the next chapter of the book.

Culture Shock

We experience culture shock when we are confronted with the vast differences between our culture and another one. At first, all the exotic sights, spicy food odors, quaint customs, etc. may seem exciting. But the excitement soon wears off. We become confused and frustrated because we do not understand all that is going on around us. This state of mind will persist until we learn some of the language and cultural practices. Then we will begin to feel more at ease.

Changes in our lives, both good and bad, cause stress. Dr T.H. Holmes has devised a scale which measures the amount of stress caused by each life-change event. For example, a change in job rates 36 points, a change in living conditions 25 points, etc. According to this study, when people experience a total of 300 Life-Change Units, they have an 80 per cent chance of coming down with a major sickness or mental illness.

When we consider all the changes involved in entering another culture, new country, language, life style, job, relationships, etc., it becomes obvious that missionaries live under tremendous pressure. On Dr Holmes' scale a new missionary's total = 400+ which gives some idea of the magnitude of stress incurred in missionary life.[2] These facts emphasize the need new missionaries have for seniors to shepherd them through the early adjustment period.

Learning a language

Adapting to a new culture involves becoming as fluent as possible in the language. We can never have an effective Christian witness unless we are able to communicate with people in their own tongue or 'heart language'. Even a stumbling attempt to speak the language helps break down people's defenses. But it is important to press on and to learn correct pronunciation, intonation, to listen to and mimic sounds and learn idioms (expressions in common usage by the people).

When I entered a new culture I diligently studied the vocabulary and attacked language learning as an academic exercise. However, I soon learned that was not the way to proceed. Equal time must be given to conversing with people. We need to learn the language from people who are native speakers of that language. We must go into the market place for language learning. The necessity of buying food is a great incentive to learning! Socializing with the people and listening to them speak the language are requirements for becoming effective communicators.

Above all, we must put aside our pride and accept being laughed at and appearing foolish. A shy person will have greater difficulty than an outgoing one in becoming fluent. However, the shy person can ask the Lord for his enabling in weakness. Missionaries should continually seek to be effective communicators in the language throughout their careers.

A basic course in linguistics is very beneficial, preferably before going out as a missionary. It is very profitable to attend one of the courses which Wycliffe Bible Translators run in several regions of the world.[3]

---

[2] Myron Loss, *Culture Shock: Dealing with Stress in Cross-Cultural Living.* Winona Lake, IND: Light & Life Press, 1983, p. 77.
[3] They can be contacted at Wycliffe Bible Translators International, 7500 W. Camp Wisdom Road, Dallas, Texas 75236, USA, or in Australia at Wycliffe Bible Translators, Graham Road, Kangaroo Ground, VIC., 3097.

Another helpful tool is a book known as LAMP, *Language Acquisition Made Practical: Field Methods for Language Learners,* by E.T. and E.S. Brewster. This material has been used effectively all over the world. The Brewsters advocate missionaries' living with a national family from the beginning so that they experience total immersion in the new culture and become bonded with the people.

Having emphasized the importance of learning the culture and language, we must not forget that *'If I speak in the tongues of mortals and of angels, but do not have love, I am a noisy gong or a clanging cymbal'* (1 Corinthians 13:1, NRSV). A dear woman who worked for many years in church ministry is an example of this truth. When the door closed in that country, she went to a Muslim land. She could not speak the language and had little knowledge of the Muslims' worldview. But the local people were drawn to her because, as they said, 'We know she loves us.' Her life spoke to the people of Christ's love more than some sermons of missionaries fluent in the language.

The missionary's life is the main message the people will read, especially during the early stages of language learning. We must model the Christian life by our attitudes and behavior or our message will lose credibility. We will consider the importance of our personal lives and relationships later in the book.

For further thought and action

1. Name some attitudes that should be avoided and others which should be adopted when entering a new culture?

2. What are the parts that make up a culture?

3. Write down some of the values that are important in your home culture.
   Note any which are unbiblical.

4. What are some of the values and beliefs in your new culture?
   Note any which are unbiblical.

5. List the changes in your life, and your family's, which entering the new culture involve.
   (No wonder you are feeling stressed!)

6. Do you feel discouraged about language learning?
   If so, check areas in which you need to change:
   pride ❏ lack of diligence ❏ being a learner ❏
   mixing with nationals ❏ seeking God's enabling ❏

4

The Gospel and Culture

A Case of Unsuitable Behavior

We must present our message and adapt our lifestyle in ways acceptable to the national people.

Samuel and Eva were sent out from their home church as missionaries to an Arab country. They had very little training or understanding of the culture to which they were going but they were very enthusiastic. Samuel was an outgoing fellow who had no trouble talking to strangers about the Lord Jesus. He would take his big, black Bible and go into the tea shops to talk with the men. He did not know much about Muslims' beliefs but he just wanted to share the gospel of Christ with them.

Samuel was rather hot headed and tended to argue with anyone who disagreed with him. The Muslims would say, 'Your Bible has been corrupted and Jesus did not die on the cross. Allah put another man there. And Allah never had relations with a woman to have a son. Allah forbid such blasphemy!'

Samuel became angry when they talked to him like that. He would reply, 'You are the ones who are blaspheming. The Koran is not God's word. Mohammed has deceived you into thinking he had revelations from God. Only Jesus Christ has come from God and he proved his deity by rising from the dead. See, you Muslims have a dead prophet but we Christians have a living Savior!' Samuel's visits in the tea shops did not last long; he had to flee to prevent the men from attacking him. But he felt happy to suffer for Jesus.

Eva was a friendly, easygoing woman. She greeted everyone she met on the streets just as she did at home. The climate was very hot so she wore her short dresses and refused to wear a head scarf. The men did not seem pleased with her and would not return her greetings. When she went into the women's quarters of the houses, they were polite but did not give her a warm welcome. She wanted to have

Bible classes with them but wondered how she could get their interest.

The senior pastor of the team with whom Samuel and Eva worked was getting unfavorable feedback about them from the national Christians. He and his wife invited them to dinner and sought to counsel them. He said to Samuel, 'Sam, I am pleased to see your eagerness to witness but I think you could be more effective in your method. You would not like it if a stranger came to your town and started ridiculing all you held sacred, would you?

I have learned that confronting people just makes them so defensive that they don't really hear what you say. You may think you have won an argument but if you have lost a person's friendship, then you cannot follow up your contact. You will find it much more profitable to befriend people, ask questions and listen to what they think is important. Then, as you pray for them you can build a meaningful relationship and opportunities will arise for you to share your faith with them. They are much more likely to absorb what you tell them. Why don't you try this approach and we will see how you get along.'

The pastor's wife took Eva out to the kitchen during their visit and had a chat with her. 'Eva, it is good to see you visiting with the people and going into their homes. But let me give you some motherly advice. The way you dress and conduct yourself is important. You see, in this culture only prostitutes wear short dresses exposing their legs, and act familiarly with men. A respectable woman dresses modestly and does not talk with men who are strangers. That's why I wear this long dress and head scarf. I only associate with men when my husband is present. I know this is different from what you are used to. But if you offend the people in these little ways, then you lose their respect and the opportunity to share Christ with them. Will you pray about this? Just ask the Lord to give you his love for the people and a willingness to change the way you do things so as not to offend them.'

We trust the couple in this story took heed of the advice of the pastor and his wife and became effective witnesses. The story shows us how easy it is to follow our own ways and lose the privilege of being heard by the people. We hinder our witness by wrong attitudes and behavior even before we begin telling the message of salvation. We must seriously consider the questions, 'What am I really here for? Am I here to impose my ways on these people? Or am I willing to make some changes in my life in order to be an effective witness for Christ?'

The Apostle Paul sets us an excellent example to follow. In his culture he had the highest credentials, status and education, *'a Hebrew of Hebrews'*. He said, *'But whatever was to my profit I now consider loss for the sake of Christ'* (Philippians 3:6,7). He was willing to put aside all his advantages and become a bond slave for Christ. We need to have a similar commitment to Christ if we want to be effective missionaries.

Paul also said, *'I have made myself a slave to all, so that I might win more of them... I have become all things to all people, that I might by all means save some'* (1 Corinthians 9:19,22, NRSV). Of course, we do not compromise our position on the basic truths of the gospel. But we can be flexible in non-essential issues. For example, we may come from a legalistic church background. We have been taught a rigid and narrow interpretation of what Christians are allowed to do on Sunday. But in the new culture, Sunday is just another day of the week. This is true in Muslim lands where Friday is the holy day for worship and rest from work. How do we adapt as missionaries? Do we insist that the church fellowship must meet on Sunday? And that the Christians should not participate in other social activities on that day? If we take such a stand, are we following biblical principles or our own cultural pressures?

We must examine every issue which arises in the same way. Is it a cultural matter which can be adapted and changed, or is it a doctrinal issue which cannot be compromised?

What is 'the gospel'

As we think about sharing the gospel, also called 'good news', a definition of terms is in order. The scriptural definition is found in 1 Corinthians 15:1-5.

> *'Now, brothers I want to remind you of the gospel I preached to you, which you received and on which you have taken your stand. By this gospel you are saved, if you hold firmly to the word I preached to you. Otherwise, you have believed in vain.*
>
> *For what I received I passed on to you as of first impor-*

tance: that Christ died for our sins according to the Scriptures, that he was buried, that he was raised on the third day according to the Scriptures, and that he appeared to Peter, and then to the twelve.'

Briefly, the gospel is the fundamental truth of the death and resurrection of Christ which provides our salvation. By faith we lay hold of the redeeming grace of God in the gospel. Then, we turn from our own rebellious ways and submit to Christ's rule in every aspect of our lives. *'And he died for all, that those who live should no longer live for themselves but for him who died for them and was raised again'* (2 Corinthians 5:15). The gospel is the means of present transformation of the lives of those who respond to it, as well as the means of eternal redemption.

Relevance of the gospel

How do we share this gospel in a culture where the values and beliefs are non-Christian? First of all, we evaluate our own worldview. Is it biblically based or still locked into our old ideas, molded by our own culture? Work through this issue before trying to change someone else's worldview. Then, we need to study and understand the worldview of the people where we live. In the previous chapter we learned that the worldview of people is determined by what is real to them. For example, if the presence of spirits of the dead is real and important to the people, can we just dismiss their view as superstition? Can we just tell them to believe in Jesus and they will not have to worry about the dead any more? No, we need to have much greater understanding of the implications of their relationship to the spirit world. When we have some grasp of that, then we may be ready to try to adapt the gospel message on that issue to their understanding.

Our motivation must be the love of Christ urging us to share the gospel. We are to show loving concern for people, concern for their earthly needs as well as for their eternal souls. Our job is not to try to convince them that we are right and they are wrong! We are responsible to witness to the saving grace of Christ. Then, we pray and trust the Holy Spirit will bring people to conviction of the truth of the gospel and to salvation.

Contextualization means making the gospel relevant within a culture, within the context of the peoples' understanding. The message of the gospel should not be altered but the method by which it is presented may need to be. For example, most tribal people do not think in abstract terms but have concrete ideas. Therefore, doctrinal teaching may be difficult for them to comprehend. But they can grasp stories such as those about Old Testament patriarchs and prophets with application to their own culture. Much of Jesus' teaching was through parables, stories of everyday life with moral application.

Seek to find an analogy in the culture to some biblical doctrine. For example, one missionary learned that in his host culture the people offered a child to their enemies after a battle, known as the 'peace child'. He was able to use this as an analogy of God's offer to us of Christ as his 'peace child'. The missionary took the people from the known to the unknown, using the analogy to explain Christ's reconciling work on the cross. In this way the people have a much better prospect of understanding and accepting gospel truth than if it is presented in a way foreign to them.

In the modern world traditional values and ways are being left behind by people as they move in great numbers to the cities. There is pressure on them to embrace materialism and secularism. This is also true in countries where economic advancement is the main drive of political leaders. Missionaries must find ways to fill the spiritual vacuum in these people's lives by making the gospel relevant to their particular needs.

Uniqueness of the gospel

We should be careful that we do not distort the gospel in order to make it acceptable, and thereby weaken the message. That would lead to **syncretism** which mixes a form of Christianity with the people's religion. This has happened in South America where some tribes take the veneration of Mary from Catholicism and accept her as their mother-earth goddess. Syncretism always fails to confront human sinfulness and our need of redemption through Christ's death.

This brings up the question, 'Is the gospel of Christ the only way to God?' Some people think that everyone is acceptable to

God if they are living the best they can under their religious system. Such an idea makes a mockery of the death of Christ. Why should he bear the sins of the world if there are other ways for human beings to be saved? The Lord Jesus himself said, *'I am the way and the truth and the life. No one comes to the Father except through me'* (John 14:6). The Apostle Peter preached, *'There is salvation in no one else, for there is no other name under heaven given among mortals by which we must be saved'* (Acts 4:12, NRSV).

Understanding and tolerance toward others is important in countries where there are different religious groups. But we must not lose sight of the uniqueness of Christ. In all religions people are seeking God, but in Christ, **God is seeking people!**

Church planting and culture

Evangelism will be the responsibility of the missionaries in areas where there are no local Christians. All the principles discussed above are important to keep in mind in order to present the gospel in a cultural context. Not all of us are gifted evangelists but we are all called to be witnesses of Christ. Our witness is to be a humble sharer of God's grace. As someone has expressed it, 'It is like one beggar telling another beggar where to find bread'. A Scripture I have found challenging and yet encouraging in witnessing is 1 Peter 3:15. *'But in your hearts set apart Christ as Lord. Always be prepared to give an answer to everyone who asks you to give the reason for the hope that you have. But do this with gentleness and respect.'* The last part is especially important when witnessing in another culture. We should never say, 'My religion is better than yours'. Such an attitude toward people of another religion will spoil our witness.

I once heard a missionary say after he had preached a sermon, 'Well, I gave them the gospel. Now it is up to them as to what they do with it.' He had delivered his soul of the message but I wondered what impact it had on the souls of his listeners! He had never gone beyond a basic, survival vocabulary in the language. His sermon made no sense to the people. Yet, he thought his explanation of the gospel was sufficient for people to whom it was a totally new concept.

We noted in the Introduction to the book that God has given

us the **ministry** and the **message** of reconciliation (2 Corinthians 5:18-20). Both are means of witnessing for Christ. Our ministries will vary; for example, preaching, teaching, healing, visiting, etc. But whatever our work, we are witnessing through our lives, attitudes and behavior. We may think of work as pre-evangelism, and our opportunities to share the message of the gospel, as evangelism.

The role of **discipling** becomes the main task of missionaries as the Holy Spirit works in people's hearts, bringing some to faith in Christ. The new believers must be established in the Word of God and taught to apply biblical truth to their lives within their own culture. Missionaries serve as parents to new converts, training and leading them in the way of the Lord.

Early in my missionary work a mission leader advised me, 'Concentrate on a few people near you. You cannot influence all the people.' I followed that advice by devoting time to our hospital staff with whom we had prolonged contact. Eventually, several of them did trust the Lord and persisted in Bible study and fellowship with other believers. Later, I realized that we had used the method of discipling stated in 2 Timothy 2:2. '...*And what you have heard from me before many witnesses entrust to faithful people who will be able to teach others as well*' (RSV).

When the local church, or community of believers, is established in an area the missionaries should step aside to become **partners** with the national leaders. The growth of the church will be stifled if the leaders are continually treated like children.

These leaders will have to struggle with making the church relevant in their own culture. They must use biblical principles for establishing the doctrines and practices of church life. Too often church leaders themselves are chosen because of their tribal or social status, rather than because of their Christian maturity. The leaders will be under pressure to run the church in old, traditional ways. It is hard for them to break with the old patterns and implement biblical principles of practice in the church.

An example of the problems in applying Scripture is a polygamous culture. What should the church leaders advise converts to do about their wives? Do they demand that the converts get rid of all but one wife? If so, what happens to the others who will have no status or means of support in the community?

There are no easy answers to such issues. Decisions must be made by the nationals who know the impact certain actions will have in their culture. Missionaries can advise about scriptural principles but should not force their decisions upon the national church.

The missionaries will ultimately become **participants** in the church life. They should be models of Christian living which the nationals can copy. They can use their skills to train and motivate the national Christians to mature in Christ. Then, the nationals in turn will become church planters and fulfill the Great Commission in their 'Jerusalem' and throughout the world.

Ministry of Prayer

The penetration of any culture by the gospel of Christ must be based on the foundation of prayer. The most important ministry missionaries can exercise at every stage of their careers is the ministry of prayer. They must pray during the early days of evangelism among an unreached people group. Then, as the work develops into a strong national church, the missionaries' role must be one of an intercessor before God for the church. The Lord Jesus himself enables us in this ministry, *'Therefore he is able to save completely those who come to God through him, because he always lives to intercede for them'* (Hebrews 7:25).

The discipline of an effective prayer ministry is difficult to maintain in busy missionary life. A missionary friend of mine served thirty years in a fruitful ministry of evangelism and church planting. When asked, 'What would you do differently if you had the time over again?' his immediate response was, 'I would pray more.' We tend to think our ministries of teaching, visiting, etc. are the main work and we cover them by prayer. But we need to view prayer, waiting upon God for his power and blessing, as the main task. Then, the other aspects of our lives and service will have an effective impact.

- Prayer must be the top priority in a missionary's life, not an optional extra. *'Without faith it is impossible to please God'* (Hebrews 11:6).
- We must live and pray in total dependence on the Lord. *'If*

you remain in me, and my words remain in you, ask what-
ever you wish, and it will be given you' (John 15:7).

● We must ask in Jesus' name, which implies his character, and is consistent with his Word, his will. *'I will do what-ever you ask in my name, so that the Son may bring glory to the Father. You may ask me for anything in my name, and I will do it'* (John 14:13,14).

● We must discern God's will in a matter and then pray, con-fident that God hears and answers the prayers of his peo-ple. *'This is the confidence we have in approaching God: that if we ask anything according to his will, he hears us. And if we know that he hears us — whatever we ask — we know that we have what we asked of him'* (1 John 5:14,15).

● We must fill our minds with the Word of God in order to pray aright. *'Do not conform any longer to the pattern of this world, but be transformed by the renewing of your mind. Then you will be able to test and approve what God's will is — his good, pleasing and perfect will'* (Romans 12:2).

● Pray in the words of Scripture, e.g. Paul's prayers for the churches in the Epistles. See Ephesians 1:15-23; 3:14-21; Colossians 1:9-12; 2 Thessalonians 1:11-12.

● We must live under the control of the Holy Spirit, in order that he may direct our praying. *'The Spirit helps us in our weakness. We do not know what we ought to pray for, but the Spirit himself intercedes for us with groans that words cannot express. And he who searches our hearts knows the mind of the Spirit, because the Spirit intercedes for the saints in accordance with God's will'* (Romans 8:26,27).

Spiritual warfare

The servants of the Lord Jesus are met by various types of oppo-sition when they seek to proclaim the gospel in cultures where Christ is not known. There is open resistance to the message, spiritual oppression upon the messengers, discouragement because of few converts and conflict with the prevailing reli-gious system. Also, demonic activity is prevalent and there are various forms of possession of people by demons. The antagonism of our arch enemy, Satan, is behind all these evil forces. The only way we can overcome such spiritual opposition to the gospel is through prevailing prayer. We must learn to use the weapons of spiritual warfare in order to pull down the strongholds of Satan.

To illustrate the evil forces working against us and our ministries, I quote from a missionary's prayer letter used by permission.

'Many people here, even Christians, do not understand the truth that Jesus came to destroy the works of the devil and that he defeated Satan at the cross. They do not understand the freedom that Christ has won for us. They believe the lies that the evil spirits put into their minds and they live in fear and bondage.

R. and M. are a couple who grew up as animists. Whenever someone in the family was sick R. & M. would consult a shaman (an occult practitioner). A sacrifice would be made to appease the spirits and traditional medicine was prescribed. Every time they did this they put themselves in bondage to these spirits. R. became ill, losing his sight and balance. At that time they were involved in a sect which promised healing. Many churches here mix biblical teaching and the occult together. This put them in further bondage. Later, they went to an evangelical church and eventually became Christians. However, their problems did not end; R.'s health did not improve.

Another missionary and I started praying for R. and M. They confessed their sin of worshipping spirits, etc. We helped them to renounce all demonic working that had been passed on to them from their ancestors. They were delivered of several spirits. Now they are experiencing much more peace and R. has regained his balance.

We continue to pray with them and for them. Sometimes it takes quite a while for a person to be completely free. Deliverance is a process and is not a short cut to maturity. The person has to learn to listen to the Word of God so that the Holy Spirit can renew his mind. He must learn the truth so that he can recognize deceiving spirits. Also, he needs to learn to be responsible for overcoming evil powers in his own life.

Pray for us missionaries in this spiritual battle. It is spiritually, emotionally and physically draining. Pray that God would protect us from attack, especially in the areas of personal safety, health and relationships. Pray that God will give us discernment to know what is *causing peoples' problems and the power of the Spirit to combat evil forces.'*

Our Part in Spiritual Warfare

- We battle from our position in Christ, not from our earthly position. *'Praise be to the God and Father of our Lord Jesus Christ, who has blessed us in the heavenly realms with every spiritual blessing in Christ'; 'And God raised us up with Christ and seated us with him in the heavenly realms in Christ Jesus'* (Ephesians 1:3; 2:6).

- We are to exercise our authority in Christ. *'All authority in heaven and on earth has been given to me. Therefore, go... And surely I am with you always, to the very end of the age'* (Matthew 28:18,20).
  'I will give you the keys of the kingdom of heaven; whatever you bind on earth will be bound in heaven, and whatever you loose on earth will be loosed in heaven' (Matthew 16:19).

- We wield our weapons in prayer for the defeat of evil powers. *'The weapons we fight with are not the weapons of the world. On the contrary, they have divine power to demolish strongholds'* (2 Corinthians 10:4).

- We claim the promises of God in his Word. *'... so is my word that goes out from my mouth; It will not return to me empty, but will accomplish what I desire and achieve the purpose for which I sent it'* (Isaiah 55:11).

- We claim the power of the blood of Christ over Satan. *'They overcame him (Satan) by the blood of the Lamb and by the word of their testimony...'* (Revelation 12:11).

- We resist the devil and draw near to God. *'Submit yourselves, then, to God. Resist the devil, and he will flee from you. Come near to God and he will come near to you'* (James 4:7-8).
  'Be self-controlled and alert. Your enemy the devil prowls around like a roaring lion looking for someone to devour. Resist him, standing firm in the faith' (1 Peter 5:8,9).

- We must be strong in the Lord and put on the whole armor of God. *'Finally, be strong in the Lord and in his mighty power. Put on the full armor of God so that you can take your stand against the devil's schemes. For our struggle is not against flesh and blood, but against the rulers, against the authorities, against the powers of this dark world and against the spiritual forces of evil in the heavenly realms'* (Ephesians 6:10-12).

For further thought and action

1. List some of the ways you acted in your home culture which would be unacceptable in your new culture. For example, the way you dress, eat, relate, etc.

2. Can you define 'the gospel'? How does it affect your every day living?

3. How would you go about making the gospel relevant to people who fear the spirits of the dead?

4. How would you respond to the statement, 'All religions are good. People should be left alone to seek God in their own way.'

5. What do you see as your role in the national church in its present development?

6. What steps do you need to take to make prayer the top priority in your life and service?

7. Keep a list in your Bible of the Scripture references regarding prayer and spiritual warfare. Review often.

8. Ask the Lord daily to make you effective in prayer and in the spiritual battle against evil.

5

Spiritual Life of the Missionary

Missionaries have high ideals and a strong commitment to the Lord. But these standards can accentuate their sense of failure if they feel they are not living an abundant Christian life.

A Case of Being too Busy

Mary came to see me after her first four-year term of missionary service. 'I wasn't the victorious, witnessing Christian I thought I should be', she said sadly. 'Finding time for prayer and Bible reading in the busy hospital work was a losing battle. I was always too busy or too tired.'

'Well, Mary, you are not alone in those struggles. Most missionaries face the same problem, especially those involved in medical ministries', I replied.

'But how can I go back to the field? I feel I have failed the Lord and failed as a missionary.'

'Firstly', I said, 'be assured that God understands the demands of a busy hospital work. You know that you are acceptable to God through his grace, not because of your performance. Let's look together at the first chapter of Ephesians and review all that God has graciously provided for us through Christ.'

After we discussed the Bible passage Mary said, 'Yes, I see that God's love for me is unconditional and is not influenced by whether I feel "spiritual" or not. But I still don't want to go back and get into the same situation of being driven by work.'

'Let's review your schedule and see what things can be changed or delegated in order for you to have more control of your life', I suggested. 'We all have to struggle with our priorities, whatever our work may be. Our time with the Lord must be at the top of the list. Then, we are able to work out our daily schedule in a reasonable way.'

Mary's problem is common to many missionaries. Time for Bible reading and prayer can be squeezed out by being too busy and tired. This leads to irritability and impatience which can damage their Christian testimony. Missionaries' attitudes and behavior have more of an impact upon the people than many sermons. Being too busy to nourish our own souls and spirits is detrimental to abundant Christian living.

Another area in which many missionaries feel frustrated is witnessing for Christ. A common teaching is that 'fruit' in the Christian life consists of souls saved. This can cause discouragement, especially in ministries where there are few visible results, such as Muslim work. In Scripture the *'fruit of the Spirit'* (Galatians 5:22), and *'fruit of righteousness'* (James 3:18 NASB), refer to Christian character which is a witness in itself. Of course, missionaries are to have a verbal witness for Christ but the saving of souls is God's business.

The sections on ministry of prayer and spiritual warfare in the previous chapter are relevant in this present discussion. We cannot live effectively under the pressures of another culture without the daily enabling of the Holy Spirit. Satan is aware of this and will try to undermine the spiritual foundation of our lives and witness. We must continually assess and rearrange our schedules to make time for the nourishment of our spiritual life.

Besides keeping ourselves spiritually fit, we must be sensitive to and caring for the needs of our fellow workers. Pastoral care of one another within the body of Christ is an important part of missionaries' responsibility. Our own interests and activities must not prevent us from being concerned for our colleagues. Some scriptural advice about this issue is: *'Serve one another in love'* (Galatians 5:13). *'And let us consider how we may spur one another on toward love and good deeds. ...let us encourage one another'* (Hebrews 10:24,25).

Maturing in Christ

When we are born again by the Holy Spirit, we tend to think that all our struggles are over. But we soon learn that we have only reached the starting line in our spiritual pilgrimage. As we submit to Christ as Lord (the boss) of our lives, we are no longer slaves to our sinful nature. We are identified with Christ in his death and burial, and are raised to new life with Him. We are no longer compelled to obey our sinful nature but are free to obey Christ (see Romans 6).

However, we find that the old, sinful nature has not been destroyed. It still asserts itself. *'I know that nothing good lives in me, that is, in my sinful nature'* (Romans 7:18). This is confirmed by Galatians 5:17, *'For the sinful nature desires what is contrary to the Spirit, and the Spirit what is contrary to the sinful nature. They are in conflict with each other, so that you do not do what you want.'*

In Romans 8 we find the glorious dimension of life we can enjoy when we are controlled by the Holy Spirit. *'You, however, are controlled not by the sinful nature but by the Spirit, if the Spirit of God lives in you'* (Romans 8:9). Our position before God is that of being new creatures in Christ. However, our daily walk is often inconsistent with our Christian position. We are in a spiritual battle as long as we are in this world. We are admonished in Scripture to *'put off your old self ... to be made new in the attitude of your minds; and to put on the new self, created to be like God in true righteousness and holiness'* (Ephesians 4:22-24). This is not a once for all transaction but a continual practice. It results in our being conformed more and more to the image of Christ.

Intellectual understanding of Scripture does not guarantee spiritual growth. *'Knowledge puffs up, but love builds up'* (1 Corinthians 8:1). I have often heard Christians longingly exclaim, 'If only I could move my head knowledge into heart experience.' This transformation takes place as we pray scriptural truth into our hearts and work it out in daily living. Our maturing in Christ is not a steady, upward line but usually a wobbly one. We find, in hindsight, that the spurts of growth have taken place in times of trials and difficulties, not during the easy times.

The idea that we will eventually become sinless as we mature spiritually is misleading. We do not arrive at that blessed position until we go to be with the Lord in heaven. Acceptance of this fact will keep us from being deceived by teaching of instant holiness or sinless perfection. In the New Testament the word 'perfect' is used for mature, complete, but not for sinlessness.

'Not that I have already obtained all this, or have already been
made perfect, but I press on to take hold of that for which
Christ Jesus took hold of me. ...All of us who are mature should
take such a view of things' (Philippians 3:12,15).

Temptation and Sin

Missionaries battle with temptation and need to understand the
difference between temptation and sin. I used to believe that if
wrong thoughts came into my mind, that was as bad as committing sinful acts. But as I renewed my mind through the
Scriptures, I realized that temptation and sin are not the same.
Evil thoughts will torment us as long as we are in this sinful
world but we must not entertain them. If we do, we give the
devil a foothold over us. We can define **temptation** as the entice-
ment to evil, and **sin** as the yielding to and committing of evil.
Even the Lord Jesus was tempted during his earthly life but he
did not yield to Satan's seduction. *'For we do not have a high
priest who is unable to sympathize with our weaknesses, but we
have one who has been tempted in every way, just as we are —
yet was without sin'* (Hebrews 4:15).

Missionaries are open to temptation as much as any
Christian. Perhaps more so, because of their location and surroundings. They are located in the front lines of the battle,
wrestling to free Satan's captives, which makes them special tar-
gets of the enemy. Also, they live in pagan, non-Christian envi-
ronments in which the presence of evil is very oppressive. They
must continually submit to God and resist the enticements of
Satan. *'Resist the devil, and he will flee from you. Come near to
God and he will come near to you'* (James 4:7,8).

A warning we need to keep in mind is, *'If you think you are
standing firm, be careful that you don't fall!'* (1 Corinthians
10:12). The Lord admonished his disciples at Gethsemane,
*'Watch and pray so that you will not fall into temptation. The
spirit is willing, but the body is weak'* (Matthew 26:41).
Christians never reach a spiritual position where they cannot be
tempted.

Satan tries to entice us to think and do evil. He wants to
defeat and discourage us in our missionary life and service. We
read in Genesis 3 that Satan tempted Eve to doubt God's **word,**

'*Did God really say...?*' And to doubt God's **judgment** upon disobedience, '*You will not surely die.*' Then, to doubt God's **goodness** because God forbad Adam and Eve to eat of one particular tree. The devil was trying to get Adam and Eve's eyes off all the good things God had provided for them in the garden, and make them desire what was forbidden. Satan was implying by his lies that what God allows is dull, unattractive, but what is forbidden is exciting and desirable. All these types of temptation continue to plague us today.

'*...for all that is in the world — the desire of the flesh, the desire of the eyes, the pride in riches — comes not from the Father but from the world*' (1 John 2:16, NRSV).

Means of Forgiveness

Our method of dealing with sin is somewhat different from handling temptation. We must take action in resisting temptation but we cannot actively remedy our sinfulness. The root of our sins is our sinful nature. The remedy for sin is not trying to become sinless, but partaking of the **grace of God**.

The first step in dealing with our sin is to **confess** and admit it before God. When we uncover and acknowledge our sin, God covers it with the blood of Jesus. But just being sorry over our sin, or that we were found out, is not enough. The Holy Spirit will convict us of our offense against God and move us to true **repentance**, which involves a change in thinking and direction, as well as sorrow over sin. John the Baptist proclaimed the need to '*Produce fruit in keeping with repentance*' (Matthew 3:8). Paul preached, '*that they should repent and turn to God and prove their repentance by their deeds*' (Acts 26:20).

Then, we must accept and believe in God's **forgiveness**. Our pride makes us feel ashamed of our sin and think that we must do something to atone for it, pray and read the Bible more, become more active in church life. But such thinking implies that the death of Christ was not quite adequate for our need and that we have to add something ourselves. That is blasphemy. The assurance of Scripture could not be more plain. '*If we confess our sins, he is faithful and just and will forgive us our sins, and purify us from all unrighteousness*' (1 John 1:9).

Of course, Satan will try to keep us in bondage to our sin.

One way he does this is to use the **tyranny of guilt** to keep us bowed down. We feel we are helpless and hopeless in our struggle with the particular sins that beset us. When Satan accuses us, it causes vague feelings of worthlessness. But when the Holy Spirit convicts us of guilt, it is about specific sins which can be dealt with by confession and repentance.

When Satan torments us with accusations about sins which have been confessed and forgiven, we must stand against his assault. *'They overcame him by the blood of the Lamb and by the word of their testimony'* (Revelation 12:11). It is sometimes helpful to do this aloud, claiming the blood of Christ over our sin and guilt, and proclaiming our word of testimony. We do not fight this battle in our own power, but through the power of God's Spirit working in us.

I have found in my own life and in counseling others that justification through faith alone is one of the most difficult concepts to accept. We feel we must add something to our salvation by our own good works. But we read in Romans 4:25, *'He (Christ) was delivered over to death for our sins and raised to life for our justification.'* Therefore, we are justified through the finished, perfect work of Christ. We are as completely justified now as we will be when we stand before God at the end of our life on earth. Jesus' blood and righteousness are our only defense now, and will be our only defense then.

This is a very liberating truth which will free us from the vain struggle of trying to make ourselves more acceptable before God by our works. Rather, our good deeds will be motivated by a heart full of gratitude to God for his gracious provision for us in Christ and our desire to please and glorify him. *'Therefore, since we have been justified through faith, we have peace with God through our Lord Jesus Christ, through whom we have gained access by faith into this grace in which we now stand'* (Romans 5:1).

Spiritual renewal

Many missionaries long and pray for revival in their own lives and ministries, as well as in the church world wide. Roy Hession was deeply affected by the East Africa revival movement. He has clearly stated the principles of renewal in his book, *My Calvary*

Road. I have been greatly blessed and challenged by his writings. The five principles are: prayer, brokenness, fullness, openness and oneness.

Revival begins with a deep dissatisfaction over the level of spiritual life in oneself and in the church generally. *'Blessed are those who hunger and thirst for righteousness, for they will be filled'* (Matthew 5:6). This must drive us to persistent **prayer** for the Spirit of God to do a new thing among his people, starting with me. *'Restore us again, O God our Savior...Will you not revive us again, that your people may rejoice in you?'* Psalm 85:4,6).

Brokenness takes place as we confess our spiritual poverty and helplessness. We must reject our pride and yield our rights to everything before God. We are humbled as we confess and repent of our sinfulness. *'Humble yourselves, therefore, under God's mighty hand, that he may lift you up in due time'* (1 Peter 5:6).

The result is the **fullness** in our hearts with the overflowing blessings of the Holy Spirit. *'But the fruit of the Spirit is love, joy, peace, patience, kindness, goodness, faithfulness, gentleness and self-control... Since we live by the Spirit, let us keep in step with the Spirit'* (Galatians 5:22,25).

Openness is the opposite of hypocrisy. It involves living in honest fellowship with God and our fellow Christians. *'But if we walk in the light, as he is in the light, we have fellowship with one another, and the blood of Jesus, his Son, purifies us from all sin'* (1 John 1:7).

Oneness with our fellow Christians is necessary for revival. We must be willing to deal with sin in every one of our relationships in order to walk in the Spirit. *'Make every effort to keep the unity of the Spirit through the bond of peace. There is one body and one Spirit — just as you were called to one hope when you were called — one Lord, one faith, one baptism; one God and Father of all, who is over all and through all and in all'* (Ephesians 4:3-6).

Our aim in praying for revival involves more than our own spiritual blessing. The ultimate goal should be for the Lord Jesus to be known and worshipped throughout the earth. *'May God be gracious to us and bless us and make his face shine upon us,*

*that your ways may be known on earth, your salvation among
all nations'* (Psalm 67:1,2).

Trials and suffering

Missionaries are not immune to the suffering and hurts common
to the human race in this fallen world. When they are going
through trials and suffering, they need to see God's sovereignty
in their circumstances. This is especially important when his
purposes seem to be hidden behind the shadows of grief and
loss.

*A young couple were working in an isolated area when their child
became critically ill. I was able to fly to their village to examine the
child. As soon as I palpated her abdomen, I feared the worst. I felt a
large, hard, nodular mass which was surely cancer. I had to tell the
parents what I had found and that it would be necessary for them to
return to their home country for treatment. They had been treating
the child for worms and this turn of events was most unexpected.
Their natural reaction was to ask, 'Why? Why would God allow this to
happen when we are just learning the language and getting involved
in ministry here? We obeyed God's call to come to this place and
now our child has cancer. Why?' I had no answer to their 'why'. I wept
with this couple over their present trouble and sought to assure them
of God's loving concern for them. I encouraged them to trust in God's
sovereign purposes for them and their child through the difficult days
ahead.*

I could identify with them in their bewilderment. I had been
through a similar experience myself early in my missionary
career. After completing language study and embarking into the
medical work, I was laid aside with a serious illness. I too struggled with, 'Why?' Why did God allow this when I had invested
all that time to learning the language and culture? Would I have
to leave the mission field? As I studied the Scriptures and wait-
ed upon the Lord, I realized I was asking the wrong question. I
learned to ask, 'What?', rather than 'Why?' What did God want
to teach me through this time of trial? This attitude delivered me
from doubt and confusion. I sought to learn lessons through it
all, even though I could not understand God's ways.

Christians are often confused when they undergo hardship

and suffering through no fault of their own. They wonder if God is displeased with them and is punishing them. These doubts arise from a lack of understanding of scriptural teaching. God always deals with us in our trials as a loving father. *'Endure trials for the sake of discipline. God is treating you as children ... but he disciplines us for our good, in order that we may share his holiness. Now discipline always seems painful rather than pleasant at the time, but later it yields the peaceful fruit of righteousness to those who have been trained by it'* (Hebrews 12:7,10,11, NRSV).

Another aspect of God's purposes for us in times of suffering is stated in 2 Corinthians 1:3,4. *'Praise be to the God and Father of our Lord Jesus Christ, the Father of compassion and the God of all comfort, who comforts us in all our troubles, so that we can comfort those in any trouble with the comfort we ourselves have received from God.'* Our life and service is enriched as we learn to know God better through our trials. Then, we are able to share some of the love and grace of God we have experienced in our trials with others who are suffering.

Of course, we will experience persecution and suffering in this world simply because we are Christ's disciples. Our Lord warned us, *'If the world hates you, keep in mind that it hated me first. ...If they persecuted me, they will persecute you also'* (John 15:18,20).

The Apostle Peter has this word of assurance for us at such times. *'Dear friends, do not be surprised at the painful trial you are suffering, as though something strange were happening to you. But rejoice that you participate in the sufferings of Christ, so that you may be overjoyed when his glory is revealed'* (1 Peter 4:12,13).

For further thought and action

1. How do you need to change your schedule in order to make time for regular Bible study and prayer?

2. Are you alert for opportunities to witness for Christ? See 1 Peter 3:15

3. What factors have been important in your maturing as a Christian?

4. Study Genesis 3:1-7. By what means does Satan tempt you to doubt God's word, his judgment, his goodness?

5. Read 1 John 2:16. What are the particular attractions of the world you need to guard against?

6. How can your fellowship with the Lord be restored when you have given in to temptation and sinned?

7. How have you handled trials which were not due to your own actions? How could you handle them in a more godly manner?

6

Personal Life of the Missionary

Many of us were raised in a family and community where love and acceptance were conditional. That is, we felt loved and accepted only if we performed in a prescribed manner. So we formed our self-image on the basis of how well we met the demands and approval others placed upon us. This affects our self-image as adults so that we are still trying to conform to the expectations of others.

Missionaries need to be secure in their sense of identity and destiny in Christ as they live in another culture. We noted in a previous chapter that their feeling of self-worth is under constant attack. Being ridiculed for lack of knowledge of the language and culture and feeling misunderstood by others cause missionaries to lose heart. We must feel secure in our position in Christ in order to survive these pressures.

Our identity in Christ

Every one of us is a unique person, made in the image of God. Christ gave his life for us and we are infinitely precious to him. Also, we will appear with him in his eternal glory! To grasp the wonder of our position in Christ, let us reflect upon some of our blessings recorded in Ephesians 1:3-14.

> 'Praise be to the God and Father of our Lord Jesus Christ, who has blessed us in the heavenly realms with **every spiritual blessing** in Christ. For he **chose** us in him... In love he **predestined** us to be **adopted** as his sons through Jesus Christ... In him we have **redemption** through his blood... **He lavished** (his grace) on us... You were marked in him with a seal, the promised **Holy Spirit**, who is a deposit guaranteeing our inheritance...'

Here we see our identity is secure in Christ and we do not have to depend upon the approval of others for our sense of self-worth.

We tend to identify ourselves with our job or role in mission work. When our status is changed for some reason we may battle with a feeling of loss of identity. I experienced this when I married and left the mission field. I can still feel the hurt of a remark made to me, 'Of course, you are no longer a missionary.' It sounded to me like, 'You are nobody.' I had to reassess my true, eternal identity in Christ which is not affected by present status.

Our **destiny** is also secure in Christ. We have been adopted into God's family and sealed with his Holy Spirit. *'Now if we are children, then we are heirs — heirs of God and co-heirs with Christ'* (Romans 8:17). With such glorious assurance, we should not feel disheartened by the threats made upon us or on our converts.

On the other hand, there is the 'self' in each of us which is the proud, independent, self-willed, self-exalting, old nature. Someone has defined sin as the 'self-indulgent-nature', s-i-n with 'I' in the center. This self is to be denied (Mark 8:34-38), to be crucified with Christ (Galatians 2:20), and crucified to the world (Galatians 6:14). We must turn from being self-centered to being Christ-centered by the Spirit's enabling.

This attitude toward our self-life is not optional if we are to be true disciples of Christ. *'If any want to become my followers, let them deny themselves and take up their cross and follow me. For those who want to save their life will lose it, and those who lose their life for my sake, and for the sake of the gospel, will save it'* (Mark 8:34,35, NRSV). Our life must be a living sacrifice to God if we want to be fruitful in missionary service. This involves sacrificing our own desires, our life-style, our time and energy, and our leisure, in order to fulfill our service to others.

Healthy mind and emotions

We learn from 1 Thessalonians 5:23 that we are tripartite beings; spirit, soul and body. All three must be nourished, not just the spirit. The soul is defined as our organ for feeling, thinking and choosing. These inner areas of our personal life are subject to oppression and discouragement when serving as missionaries.

How should we handle potentially harmful emotions and thoughts? Many missionaries tend to suppress or deny their emotions, thinking that is the spiritual way to handle them. Unfortunately, positive feelings are involved, as well as negative ones. Joy and peace are lost in the process. We must learn to acknowledge and assess our emotions. Then, we can deal with them constructively. Some emotions should be expressed to other people, such as love and gratitude. Others are best shared only with the Lord, such as most anger and hurts. We need to find out what or who triggers negative emotions, and learn how to handle those situations in a more godly manner. It may be necessary to deal with the issue which provokes the emotion but only after we have regained our composure. We are admonished in Scripture to be positive; *'Be joyful always; pray continually; give thanks in all circumstances, for this is God's will for you in Christ Jesus'* (1 Thessalonians 5:16-18).

Loneliness is commonly experienced by both married and single missionaries. We may lack meaningful fellowship with others of like mind. The companionship of the Holy Spirit is the privilege of every Christian. We need to cultivate the sense of the Spirit's indwelling presence as recorded in John 14:16,17,26. We should think about the good things we do have and avoid longing for things we lack. Missionaries can do a great service by caring for, and sharing with, one another. In caring for another's need we lose our own sense of emptiness.

Missionaries and their children are exposed to real dangers. It is natural to experience **fear** and **anxiety** in circumstances which may arise, such as robbery, assault, being taken hostage, physical attack by fanatical opponents, and being maligned as foreigners. But when we allow our fears to become obsessive and uncontrolled, we lose our peace of mind. Some people may develop prolonged, deep seated fears which are not in keeping with the circumstances. They will need special attention by a doctor or psychologist.

When we experience these emotions we need to meditate upon scriptural promises and change our thought patterns. One such passage is Philippians 4:6,7. *'Do not be anxious about any-*

thing, but in everything, by prayer and petition, with thanks-giving, present your requests to God. And the peace of God, which transcends all understanding, will guard your hearts and your minds in Christ Jesus.'

I certainly struggled with personal fears on the mission field. During language study in the capital city, I lived in a large compound made up of three houses and an office/school building. In every large city in developing countries there are numerous poor people, beggars and thieves.

One night I was awakened by the sound of gun shots. I sat up and looked outside to see what was going on. There was scuffling inside the house and more gun shots. The husband of the family in the same house had been awakened by a thief and was trying to grab him. Another thief outside had a gun and they both ran off when the missionary gave chase. We looked around to see what damage was done. There was a bullet hole just below the window where my bed was. If I had raised myself up sooner to see what was happening I might have unnerved them and been shot.

Just two months later the house was occupied by three single women when thieves broke in again. When I heard the noise, I got up and used a broom handle to chase them out. One of the thieves had a knife and slashed a missionary on the arm. I sewed her wound and we tried to get back to sleep. After this incident a watchman was employed to walk around the compound at night and hopefully, ward off thieves.

I had handled the crises of the thieves fearlessly but afterward had a **post-traumatic reaction.** Every evening as darkness fell I would become apprehensive and feel cold shivers running down my spine. Every little noise during the night would cause me to become hyper-vigilant, waiting to hear if someone was trying to break into the house. The adrenalin was rushing through my body which made sleep impossible. I tried praying through the night, but when I did I was too tired for language study the next day. Also, I felt doubtful that the Lord was caring for and protecting us from thieves. I would have prescribed a nightly sedative for someone else in this situation. But I found it difficult to do that for myself.

These experiences brought to the surface some of my childhood fears which I had out grown but still affected me. I knew the enemy, Satan, would love to immobilize me with fear so that I would break down and have to return home. Finally, instead of doubting and debating with the Lord, I told him I trusted him and knew he had allowed this situation for my growth. I vowed that I was willing to risk the danger of thieves if that was involved in the spread of the gospel in that land. And I came to the same position as Job, *'Though he slay me, yet will I hope in him'* (Job 13:15).

However, the fearful reactions persisted until I went to a country mission station for a weekend visit. There the cycle of night time fears was broken by my being away from the situation which had provoked it. I was able to return to the city to continue language study.

The couple involved in the first incident with thieves was not so fortunate. They were sent to a distant village where they lived alone among the people. The wife had not recovered from the unnerving break-in by thieves and was fearful of all around her. It soon became apparent to her husband that she could not cope, so he brought her back to the capital city. By the time they arrived, the wife had completely broken down, screaming uncontrollably at night. We had to evacuate the family back to their home country for treatment. This case illustrates the need for sensitive pastoral care of missionaries to prevent them from being stressed beyond their endurance. (Pastoral care will be discussed in Part Two.)

Anger is commonly provoked by situations and people's actions over which we have no control. Scripture grants a place for righteous anger against injustice and evil, but adds a caution, *'In your anger do not sin. Do not let the sun go down while you are still angry, and do not give the devil a foothold'* (Ephesians 4:26,27). Our angry reactions are often due to hurt pride and thwarted self-will. If these sinful reactions are not dealt with, they lead to smoldering resentment and bitterness. The writer of Hebrews warns us, *'See to it that no one misses the grace of God and that no bitter root grows up to cause trouble and defile many'* (Hebrews 12:15).

Bitterness in the heart is accompanied by an **unforgiving spirit.** We nurse our wounds, justify our bitterness, and heap judgment upon those whom we feel have caused our hurts. We cannot forgive someone who has wronged us so much. This attitude can immobilize us from enjoying life and being effective in ministry. We must follow the scriptural exhortation, *'Bear with each other and forgive whatever grievances you may have against one another. Forgive as the Lord forgave you'* (Colossians 3:13). That includes forgiving ourselves which is often a real struggle.

Missionaries can become **discouraged,** especially when there are no tangible results for their labor. Other causes of discouragement are disappointment over converts who become engrossed in sin and those who become apathetic toward the Lord. I found it helpful in these situations to keep informed and prayerful about God's work in other places. When we look beyond our own area, we are encouraged by the response to the gospel in other parts of the world.

Doubts and discouragements can lead to **depression.** This condition is experienced by most missionaries at some time in their career. Often it is aggravated by lack of sleep, fatigue, illness, etc. However, if it persists or deepens to prolonged feelings of hopelessness and worthlessness, treatment by a Christian mental health specialist must be sought. All of the above emotions can cause doubts. Am I in God's will? Does he know and care? A meaningful verse of Scripture for such occasions is, *'May our Lord Jesus Christ himself and God our Father, who loved us and by his grace gave us eternal encouragement and good hope, encourage your hearts and strengthen you in every good deed and word'* (2 Thessalonians 2:16,17).

Sexuality

One area of life in which we are most vulnerable is our sexuality. Missionaries are not above temptation in this area, including adultery, homosexuality, and other sexual perversions. In writing to the Corinthian church, Paul said about such practices, *'And that is what some of your were'* (1 Corinthians 6:11).

In fact, missionaries are under greater attack in this area than when in the homeland. They may live in an place where nudity is common, which can be a problem, especially for men. The customs of the people may involve loose relationships between the sexes and they expect the missionaries to live the same type

of life. Other circumstances, such as tiredness, sickness and separation from one's spouse, may thwart fulfillment in marriage
and increase sexual temptation. Single missionaries have to
struggle with their own sexual longings and temptations.

The largest sex organ in the body, male and female, is the
brain. It is the channel through which all the things of the world
are processed. Sexual fantasies are produced in the brain and
fed by the mind and imagination. The subconscious mind is like
a computer's memory system. It can recall all kinds of data with
which we have filled it, good and bad. Therefore, the battle in
sexual temptation takes place primarily in the mind. The male is
sexually aroused by what he sees; the brain stores those images
and can give an instant replay like a video recorder. Therefore,
men need to keep a tight rein on what they allow their eyes to
dwell upon. On the other hand, females are sexually aroused
through caresses of their body and romantic imagining. They
must be careful that friendly touching and reading romantic lit-
erature do not get out of control.

The following are some principles for handling sexual temptation and sin.

- Guard what we allow our minds to dwell upon; continually renew our minds with biblical truth.
- Keep our hearts resting in the peace of Christ, so that we
  are not driven by evil thoughts and acts.
- Change our objective to pleasing and glorifying God in our
  private life, rather than to gratifying self.
- Sexual sin must be handled like any sin, confession and
  repentance. There is no hierarchy of sin with God.
  However, there are social implications to sexual sin which
  we must resolve.
- God does not want us enslaved; but he knows our background experiences, temptations, areas of weakness, physical make-up.
- We may see our sexual urges as the biggest obstacle in our
  Christian life. God may see self-righteousness and pride as
  more harmful.
- God has his program for reshaping our lives. Like untying
  a tangled fishing line, some knots have to be untangled
  before others can be.

● Socialize more; fantasize less. It is important to build healthy relationships and get outside of ourselves. The main battle is in the mind, purity in one's thought-life.

'It is God's will that you should be sanctified: that you should avoid sexual immorality; that each of you should learn to control his [or her] own body in a way that is holy and honorable, not in passionate lust like the heathen, who do not know God...For God did not call us to be impure, but to live a holy life' (1 Thessalonians 4:3-5,7).

Stress and Burnout

Busy missionaries often feel they are constantly running and cannot stop. **Stress** has been called the 'hurry' disease. There is a healthy amount of stress which is necessary to keep us from falling into a heap. But when we become hyperactive, over engaged mentally and emotionally, then we are experiencing a harmful, overload of stress. This results in anxiety, insomnia, inability to relax. When we find ourselves in this state we must *'come apart and rest awhile'* as Christ advised his disciples (Mark 6:31). If we fail to do this, we will 'come apart' emotionally! It is important to review our activities in order to change any unrealistic goals, to see what jobs could be delegated, to learn to relax and pursue hobbies.

Burnout, on the other hand, causes us to become discouraged, emotionally withdrawn and feel hopeless about life and our ministry. It is particularly common after a demanding assignment, or at the end of a term of service. I experienced this at the end of my first four-year term. I was worn out physically, felt mentally and emotionally drained and spiritually dry. I thought life would never be worth living again and felt uncertain whether God knew or cared about my condition. Recovery requires a long break from the work, and time for physical, emotional and spiritual renewal. Other Christians can help us as we share our problems with them. Most of all at such times, we must be waiting upon the Lord to renew and encourage us. *'May the God of hope fill you with all joy and peace as you trust in him, so that you may overflow with hope by the power of the Holy Spirit'* (Romans 15:13).

A few missionaries display deep seated emotional and mental symptoms, often present before mission field experience. Such problems emphasize the necessity of psychological assessment and counseling of all missionary applicants. (This is discussed in Part Two of the book.) However, even the best preparation and care does not assure that old problems will not arise again. Missionaries may struggle with internal stresses due to childhood trauma, a broken home background, emotional deprivation, an alcoholic parent, etc. They will need professional counseling, preferably with one who is a mature Christian familiar with the pressures of missionary life. This will enable the missionaries to resolve old conflicts and enable them to handle the added stresses of living and working cross-culturally.

Handling Mental/Emotional Conflicts

Some attitudes to adapt and actions to take in order to maintain mental and emotional health are:

- Express positive feelings more often. *'Rejoice in the Lord always. I will say it again: Rejoice!'* (Philippians 4:4).
- Cast negative feelings on the Lord (Philippians 4:6,7).
- Renew the mind daily with the word of God (Romans 12:2).
- Make every thought captive to obey Christ (2 Corinthians 10:5).
- Prayerfully seek the fruit of the Spirit, *'love'*, *'joy'*, *'peace'*, etc. (Galatians 5:22).
- Cultivate a sense of humor and ability to laugh at oneself (Proverbs 15:13; 17:22).
- Seek counsel of others and share needs with them. *'Carry each other's burdens, and in this way you will fulfil the law of Christ'* (Galatians 6:2).
- Delight in God's forgiveness; pray for a forgiving spirit toward others (Matthew 6:14,15).
- Resist the Devil, don't give him a foothold in the mind (1 Peter 5:6-10).

Physical aspects of life

'We have this treasure [the gospel] in jars of clay [our mortal bodies]' (2 Corinthians 4:7).

A complete medical check-up is important in preparation for missionary service and during home leave. Living in another culture often involves exposure to diseases for which the missionary has no immunity. It is necessary to have all the immunizations advised for the part of the world to which the missionary is going. Also, to have booster vaccines when indicated and take malaria prevention tablets as prescribed for that area. A relevant proverb says, 'An ounce of prevention is worth a pound of cure'. If the missionary plans to work in a remote area, it is wise to have a dental check-up and take an extra pair of prescription eye glasses, and an adequate supply of any prescription drugs needed for members of the family.

We should observe rules of healthy and clean living wherever we live. That includes a balanced diet, adequate sleep and exercise. Also, we must teach our children about special precautions to take, e.g. wash hands before eating food, drink only boiled water and milk. A clean, safe water supply and proper disposal of waste are essential. Fly screens on the windows and mosquito nets over the beds are mandatory in areas where insect transmitted diseases, such as malaria, are prevalent. We should give our bodies time to adjust and take adequate fluids and rest when going into a hot, humid climate or into a high altitude.

We need to be aware of the world-wide prevalence of HIV (AIDS). We should take precautions about having injections and blood transfusions, making sure the equipment is properly sterilized. Missionaries going to undeveloped areas should take a supply of sterile syringes and needles with them. Many mission agencies are now setting up blood bank information about their members, i.e. blood group, HIV and hepatitis B status. Then, when a missionary needs a transfusion, a safe donor can be found among the missionaries in the region.

Even with all the precautions, we and family members are likely to become ill at some time. We must use common sense and get proper treatment and rest. We are tempted to drag ourselves around trying to work but this is unproductive. It is a good time for learning that we are not indispensable and for learning to depend more upon the Lord, less upon our own strength. In prolonged illness we can easily become depressed. Such feelings are usually part of the illness and will recede as we regain our health.

Family planning is a vital issue on the mission field. Pregnancy takes its toll on a woman's welfare and energy. Some vaccinations should be avoided during pregnancy. Steps should be taken to prevent pregnancy during the early adjustment on the field. Delivery and post-natal care present their own problems in areas which are isolated or have poor medical facilities. If it is necessary for the mother to go to a larger center for delivery, the husband is left with the added load of caring for the family. The addition of a child is a wonderful gift but there is a need for wise planning in mission field circumstances.

A basic medical kit is useful for treatment of minor symptoms. For example, medications for headaches, pain, fever, coughs and colds, vomiting and diarrhea. Also antibiotics for infections, drugs for treating malaria (different from tablets taken for prevention), antiseptic and dressings for wounds and skin lotions. A doctor can advise you as to what is available in your locality which can be used in such a medical kit. Helpful books for basic health care and treatment of common illnesses should be taken to the field, as well as a First Aid manual.[1]

---

[1] A book which I highly recommend for missionaries living in isolated areas is *Where There is No Doctor* by David Werner, published by The Hesperian Foundation, PO Box 1692, Palo Alto, CA 94302; available in several languages including English, Spanish, Swahili and Portuguese.

For further thought and action

1. What false securities of the world do you tend to depend upon? Example: money, job, social status, etc.

2. State in your own words what you have learned about your true, eternal identity in Christ.

3. In what areas of your life do you need to implement change in order to be a true disciple of Jesus Christ? For example, use of time, thought life, attitudes, etc.

4. Which of the emotions/mental states discussed in this chapter are of particular concern to you? How can you handle them in a more positive way?

5. What principles of staying healthy have you learned from this chapter? How can you put them into practice in your locality?

7

Inter-Personal Relationships

Relationships among missionaries are often the strongest and most enriching of a life time. The stresses common to missionary life give them an understanding and appreciation for each other that is rare in ordinary life. Their hearts are bound together in prayer and fellowship as they face danger, grief, opposition, and see the Lord move on their behalf. They also share the encouraging aspects of the work, such as conversions and spiritual growth of the national church.

Differences among missionaries

In spite of the above, many missionaries leave their work and return to their home country because of conflict with other missionaries. There are misunderstandings between missionaries and nationals but that is expected and allowance is made for their differences. The main source of tension for missionaries is differences among themselves, such as personalities, nationalities, family backgrounds, doctrinal preferences, philosophies of ministry, gender and age. These are all potential grounds for misunderstandings unless an effort is made to recognize and accept differences among colleagues.

Different personalities can complement each other and make various contributions to the missionary task. In discussions and making decisions all members must be allowed to express their ideas on an issue. Then, the leadership will be responsible for formulating strategy and everyone must cooperate in carrying it out.

Differences among members can result in tension within ministry teams. Satan will seek to magnify these issues and sow seeds of dissension in any spiritual work. We must diligently obey the scriptural admonition, *'Make every effort to keep the unity of the Spirit through the bond of peace'* (Ephesians 4:3). Attention to this matter is vital for missionaries' effective witness and also for establishing national churches which will demonstrate the unity of the Spirit.

Communication Skills

Harmony among missionaries can be promoted by better communication skills in relating to each other. Such skills are essential for preventing conflict and for resolving it in a positive manner. There is much emphasis on communicating cross-culturally but little attention is paid to the importance of clear communication among missionaries. We should express clearly what we mean to say and listen carefully to what the other person is saying. Also, it is important to pick up nonverbal clues, such as body language and attitudes. Studies indicate that the components of communication are made up of attitude 55 per cent, non-verbal aspects 38 per cent, and words we speak only seven per cent. This means we must try to harmonize these three elements in order to be effective communicators.

Let us consider the part that attitude plays in our communicating. Attitude is defined as 'viewpoint, manner, disposition'. We may use kind words but cancel their effect by frowning and speaking harshly. This demonstrates how necessary it is to have right attitudes toward others in order to communicate well. As we mentioned previously, we must care for and encourage one another. That is how we build and maintain the team spirit of those with whom we work. A Scripture portion which has always stirred me about this issue is Philippians 2:3-5. *'Do nothing out of selfish ambition or vain conceit, but in humility consider others better than yourselves. Each of you should look not only to your own interests, but also to the interests of others. Your attitude should be the same as that of Christ Jesus.'* That is a challenge!

Inter-personal Conflict

Mission and team leaders should do all they can to help missionaries relate well to each other. Those in leadership need to be aware of conflicts and serve as mediators before situations get too bad to remedy. Seminars, on the field and at home, are helpful for teaching and reinforcing good communication skills and conflict resolution.

Accepting and respecting others even though we disagree with their views is essential. Missionaries know this truth in theory but it is easy to lose sight of it in the heat of personal conflict. For example, some Christians feel strongly that Sunday is a special day for preaching, worshipping and reading God's word. Others think that every day is a day for worshipping, reading the Bible and proclaiming the gospel. We found in medical work, which must function seven days a week, that other members of the mission team were critical of us. We in turn, became resentful of those who sat around in their Sunday best clothes all day while we were ministering to people's needs. Those on both sides must make allowances for the others in order to prevent the different views and ministries from becoming a source of conflict. *'If it is possible, as far as it depends on you, live at peace with everyone'* (Romans 12:18).

Missionaries may have wrong goals in relating to others. Some may seem to be driven by a desire to be right all the time. They tend to manipulate situations and people to make others comply with their way. On the other hand, some may be motivated by a need for approval. Withdrawing from conflict is their means of achieving their goal. We should become aware of our strategy in handling conflict. The way we react may require reassessment and change in order to handle conflict in biblical ways. Neither backing off about every issue, nor demanding everyone always agree with us are mature ways of handling differences.

Our differences provide opportunities to broaden our understanding of others and to mature us in relationships. If there is bitterness and an unforgiving spirit it must be dealt with. We must confess such wrong attitudes and pray for the other person involved. This leads to inner release, and freedom to minister to others with whom we differ. *'Therefore let us stop passing judgment on one another... Let us therefore make every effort to do what leads to peace and to mutual edification'* (Romans 14:13,19).

Some causes of conflict

The following actions and attitudes can cause confusion and conflict in relationships:

- Rejection of a person leads to mistrust.
- Lack of openness in sharing, unresolved negative feelings, and pride.
- Differences in personality, nationality, accents, gender, doctrinal position, age, etc.
- Misunderstandings not dealt with; small matters become enlarged.
- An unforgiving attitude.
- Provocative statements and accusations.
- Communication failure, or breakdown.
- Persons with different objectives, or styles of ministry; e.g. one church worker wants to run things, another wants nationals in control.
- Failure to realize that unity does not demand uniformity of opinions.
- Failure to appreciate that diversity of gifts and methods strengthens the ministry.

Resolving Conflict

The following are some principles for preventing and resolving conflicts.

- Submit to one another (Ephesians 5:21).
- Speak the truth in love (Ephesians 4:15).
- Respect and accept the other person; a bond of trust is essential for resolution (Romans 15:7).
- Pray for the other person; try to see his/her view point.
- Pray for timing of discussion, so both parties are prepared.
- Learn to say, 'I am sorry', 'I was wrong'; without adding, 'but you...'
- Clarify objectives of each person; back off if the discussion becomes a struggle of wills.
- Avoid confrontational positions, such as accusations against other persons, bringing up old grievances.
- Stick to the present issue, get all the relevant facts.
- Seek solution to differences, without compromising princi-

ples.

- Learn the enrichment that resolving a conflict can bring to a relationship.
- Keep the lines of communication open. Make a practice of talking **to** people, rather than **about** them.

'Bear with each other and forgive whatever grievances you may have against one another. Forgive as the Lord forgave you' (Colossians 3:13).

A **mediator** has an important role to play in many cultures and the use of such means of solving differences is crucial. The team leader, as a neutral party, can use the following means to mediate in a conflict.

- Identify areas of rejection, and wrong attitudes in each party.
- Assess the objectives of each party; seek change where they are in opposition.
- Identify wrong behavioral patterns of each person.
- Break issues into smaller units which can be dealt with one at time.
- Help both parties improve communication skills.
- Seek apology and forgiveness from both sides; have the parties pray together.

'A soft answer turns away wrath, but a harsh word stirs up anger... Those who are hot-tempered stir up strife, but those who are slow to anger calm contention' (Proverbs 15:1,18, NRSV).

Case Study:

Think through the issues in the following situation. Seek to apply biblical principles and ideas in this chapter. Then, offer solutions for the potential conflict between the characters as you answer the questions at the end.

Martha An older woman who has been a pioneer missionary, active in evangelism, church planting, and discipling local people. She is fluent in the language, at home in the culture, and has excellent rapport with the national people of Mumbo who call her 'Mother'.

She comes from a conservative, traditional Asian society where elders are honored. She attended a fundamental Baptist Bible College and Teacher Training in the 1950's before missiology was an art.

Andrew A new American missionary, trained in theology and missiology, recently graduated. He comes from a large, liberal Methodist church where technology and visual props are used in teaching. His generation has little respect for elders or authority.

He has had six months of language study, and is eager to contextualize his preaching. He has recently been sent to Mumbo to teach in the Bible School.

Yacob A student in the Bible school, befriends Andrew, helps him settle. Introduces him to the officials and shop keepers in town. After a few days Yacob complains to Andrew about Martha, saying she is maternalistic, bossy, and has too much power in the local church. He says, 'We want to run the church our own way.'

Questions on Case Study:

1. What do you see as potential problem areas between Martha and Andrew?

2. What positive attitudes should Andrew seek to develop toward Martha?

3. How is Martha likely to react to Andrew's arrival at Mumbo? What positive attitudes would she need to adopt toward him?

4. How should Andrew handle Yacob's complaints about Martha?

5. What other information would you like to know about the characters, e.g. Yacob's spiritual condition and standing in the church?

6. What preventive action could a mission/team leader take in such a situation?

7. What response should a mission/team leader make to a letter of complaint from Andrew about Martha?

For further thought and action

1. What are some of the differences in missionaries discussed in this chapter which can cause misunderstandings?

2. How does our attitude affect our communication in relationships?

3. What areas of Christian doctrine might be the basis of conflict among missionaries?

4. List some of the factors that cause inter-personal conflicts.

5. What are some of the principles for resolving conflicts?

6. How can a team leader help resolve conflict between team members?

8

Marriage Relationship and Family Life

A Case of Disharmony

James and Ruth had a stressful term on the mission field. Harmful attitudes and behavior in relating to each other were intensified under the pressures of missionary life. James was the only member of the team who could do mechanical and electrical maintenance on a large hospital compound. This meant that he was continually called out for urgent jobs and spent little time with the family. Ruth saw all that needed to be done in their own home and family. She felt resentful that James seemed to devote so little time to her and the children.

Ruth was a clever, quick witted lady, articulate in expressing her thoughts and feelings. James, on the other hand, was much slower at thinking and responding. He had never learned to express his thoughts or feelings. When a decision had to be made James would think about it but fail to take action. Ruth would grow impatient in waiting for him to take the lead. Finally, she would make a decision and act upon it. James felt threatened by his clever wife and unable to match her in an argument. So, he found it easier to withdraw, rather than confront her. Although Ruth was getting her way, she felt dissatisfied with the lack of leadership by her husband in the marriage and family life. Their sexual relationship reflected the conflict in other areas of their life.

The emphasis in counseling them was to help each one to understand their own strengths and weaknesses, as well as those of their spouse. Also, to help them minister to the other's need, rather than manipulating their partner to fulfill their own need. The greatest difficulty for them was to accept the other with their differences. They had to acknowledge that neither was right or wrong, they just had different personalities.

Ruth was challenged to work on restraining her quick tongue. She was encouraged to draw out her husband and to help him express himself more readily. James had to commit himself to painful change as he had been taking the easy way out. He was encouraged to work at verbal expression of his thoughts and feelings and to exercise his responsibility in decision making in the family. Needless to say, this couple did not change old patterns overnight. They had a long, difficult road to travel in order to change their relating patterns and means of resolving conflict to constructive ones.

The relationship between husband and wife among Christians is often derived from their culture, rather than from biblical teaching. As missionaries, we must reassess our own marriages and family life in the light of Scripture. We must be willing to change our attitudes, patterns of behavior and manner of relating to each other, whatever our cultural background. The basis of the relationship must be, *'Submit to one another out of reverence for Christ'* (Ephesians 5:21). From this foundation we can move on to wives submitting in voluntary selflessness to their husbands as the church submits to Christ. And husbands, to loving their wives with the sacrificial love with which Christ loves the church. Both partners in the relationship must ask, *'What are my responsibilities in marriage?'* rather than, *'What are my rights?'* (see Ephesians 5:21-33) Biblical marriage is of major importance in another culture since it is a picture of the relationship between Christ and the church.

Pressures on the marriage

Missionaries' marriages are subject to the same pressures as in the homeland, plus the extra strain on both partners caused by cross-cultural living. The following are some of the stresses which affect marriages:

● Both partners face tremendous adjustments in the early days of learning a new culture and language. Each must be sensitive to the other's struggles and seek to encourage one another. One partner may be an extroverted person who enjoys mixing with new people. The other may be introverted and battle with making new contacts. One may be quicker at picking up the language than the other. This must never be allowed to become an issue of competition between them.

● The work demands upon the husband's time can tend to decrease his input to the family. He may be the only one able to do a job when there are staff shortages. Also, it may be necessary for him to be separated from the family if he has to travel to other locations for ministry. He will have to struggle with his priorities in order to fulfill his responsibilities as husband and father. It is important for the husband to share the spiritual aspects of ministry with his wife so that she feels part of the team.

● Wives struggle with the tensions between the roles of wife and mother, and the missionary task. Home making and child care without modern conveniences deplete their energy and time in less developed areas. Then, they may feel guilty about how little energy and time is left to spend in language learning, visitation, etc. All the responsibility for the family and the work falls upon the women when their husbands are absent. They may battle with loneliness, fear, insecurity and resentment.

● The stresses of the culture and work can hinder communication between husband and wife. They will be tempted to speak to each other only on a superficial level, such as the day's activities. They must make an effort to maintain a meaningful level of communication, taking time to share their personal needs and pleasures.

● A busy life, fatigue, illness, lack of privacy and separation, care of the children all exert pressure upon the marriage. These situations may lead to break down in communication, tensions in sexual relations, and inability to resolve conflict. The same principles for resolving conflict as listed in Chapter 7 should be applied in the marriage relationship.

Marriage enrichment

Marriage is such an important area in the life and witness of missionaries that the enrichment of it cannot be over-emphasized. Of course, any tension in the marriage will spill over into the family and into the ministry. The people among whom the family live will watch how husband and wife relate to each other. Their Christian witness will be greatly impaired if there is conflict, shouting and bad behavior toward each other. However, if they demonstrate Christ's love and care for each other in the home, that will have far greater impact than any number of sermons. One missionary wife said she could not have coped with their isolated situation without the companionship of her husband who she describes as her best friend. Such a marriage would certainly commend the gospel, portraying the relationship of Christ and his church to the national people.

It is important for missionaries to acknowledge their problems and seek counsel. Counseling should help couples become more aware of areas where they may be failing their partners. The counselor can use this time as an opportunity for marriage building. Generally, suggestions need to be made to husbands of ways they can be more thoughtful and caring of their wives. Wives may need to find ways in which they could be more pleasant and supportive of their husband's needs. Marriage Enrichment weekends run by reputable groups are recommended. These seminars give married couples directives, provide time for listening to each other, and assessing the state of their marriage. There is a Personal Inventory for husbands and wives at the end of this chapter. It will help improve the marriage relationship if both partners mark it prayerfully and honestly. Then, they can discuss it together.

Family Life

Family life is of the utmost importance in missionary endeavor. It can be the source of much joy and enrichment, or much sorrow if personal nurturing of the children is neglected. Problems within a family can be a major factor in their having to leave the mission field.

Before embarking upon missionary life, the parents should discuss with each of the children what will be involved in living in another culture. They will not understand it all but they should feel they are part of the decision making process. Children will react differently to moving to another country, depending on their personality. Some will be excited and eager, others will be fearful and reluctant to face such change. Separation from familiar friends, school and extended family cause much anxiety in children. The parents must be sensitive to each child's different needs in preparation for going and in the adjustment period in a new country.

Children need special attention in orientation to the new culture. They need help in developing positive attitudes toward the people and culture. They should be encouraged to learn the language and to mix with the national children. Issues of being a foreigner, being the 'odd one' will need to be addressed. Parents can help older children balance their position as 'third culture kids' — a mixture of their home culture and the host culture. The advantages of becoming bilingual and bicultural should be emphasized to prevent any feelings of being deprived because they live in a foreign culture. This is important for teenagers as some rebel about life as 'missionary kids', and face new problems when they return to their home country for higher education.

Family life, and that of the extended family, is the foundation of most cultures and highly valued. Therefore, it is essential for missionaries to view family life as a high priority, not something tacked on to 'the work'. Generally the mother is the main care giver for the children so the father must make time in his schedule for his role in family life. In families which are separated part of the time, both parents should use well the time they do have together. This situation arises when the husband is absent in some type of ministry, or the children are away at school.

It is desirable to have a balance in the home between openness for hospitality and ministry to nationals, but guarding some privacy for the family. Children will be resentful if they feel they are strangers in their own home and that the nationals are more important. Children are wonderful 'door openers' themselves as most cultures are family oriented. Nationals and missionaries have mutual interests in the area of children and family life and this can lead to greater understanding between them.

Parents should agree about how they **discipline** their children. If one parent is harsh and the other is permissive in this area, children will favor the latter. They may use this difference to bring division between the parents, playing one against the other. Parents must be consistent in their discipline, motivated by love and concern for the children's welfare, not by anger.

The parents' **roles** as father and mother are important to the children's development. The boys will look to their father as a role model for their own masculinity and for the formation of their adult role as a husband and father. The girls will largely follow their mother's example in forming their own femininity and later becoming a wife and mother. Of course, the children also base their views of the opposite sex upon their parents. In the home, patterns are set for both the present and the adult life of the children. No ministry is more important than that of wise, godly parenting.

The matter of the **education** of the children should be thoroughly looked into by parents. They may choose to home school their children in the early grades. Others will send primary age children to the local schools. These may be quite adequate, even though they are taught in another language. Secondary school age children may have to be sent to a larger center for schooling. It may be necessary for them to live with relatives, friends, or in boarding school, away from their family. This situation will require special care by the parents to assure the children of their love and to make the most of the time together when the children are at home. The abilities and personality of each child need consideration in making these decisions about education.

We are unable to address in depth all issues which missionaries' children and their families face. Further information on the subject can be found in the books by M. Foyle and K.S. and M.L. O'Donnell in the 'Suggested Reading' list at the end of this book.

Personal Inventory for Husbands and Wives

In marriage, as in every area of life, we need to regularly evaluate our attitudes and behavior. After the early joy of romance, we may tend to take our partner for granted and fall into hurtful patterns of relating to one another. It is helpful to periodically use a check list such as the one below. Each partner should use the personal inventory privately and honestly, then discuss together areas needing improvement and means of implementing change.

1. What areas of our family life need to be changed in order to make Christ Lord of all?

❏ family devotional time
❏ use of leisure
❏ use of finance
❏ loving, consistent discipline of children
❏ training of children
❏ priorities of family time vs. ministry time

2. Are there areas in which I have failed to leave my former way of life? e.g. selfish interests, prejudices, pressures from my parents

3. Are there areas in which I have failed to be united to my partner? e.g. pre-eminently, exclusively. (Genesis 2:24)

4. Are there ways in which I tend to belittle or ignore my partner, privately or publicly?

5. What loving attitudes and actions toward my partner need to be restored? (It may help to think over your courting days.)

6. How can I act more responsibly in fulfilling my biblical role as a husband? e.g. *'Husbands, love your wives ... He who loves his wife loves himself.'* (Ephesians 5:25-28)

7. How can I act more responsibly in fulfilling my biblical role as a wife? e.g. *'Wives, submit to your own husband, as to the Lord.'* (Ephesians 5:22)

8. In what ways do I need to improve my communication with my partner?
❏ level of communication (self-revelation, not just plans for the day)
❏ attentive listening (not just waiting for my next point)
❏ right timing (especially in discussion of disagreements)
❏ loving, accepting, non-judgmental attitudes
❏ forgiving and forgetting old hurts

9. How do I tend to manipulate my partner to get my own way?
❏ clam up and pout ❏ vent anger and shout
❏ nagging ❏ use tears ❏ insincere flattery
❏ use partner's past failings for leverage
❏ use sex to bargain ❏ refuse sex to punish

10. How do I need to change the above behavior in order to minister to my partner?
- ❏ acknowledge and share feelings without blaming my spouse
- ❏ seek to resolve differences
- ❏ offer forgiveness readily
- ❏ practice saying 'I am sorry' and 'I was wrong'
- ❏ not adding, 'but you...'
- ❏ seek to meet partner's sexual needs
- ❏ use partner's weaknesses for prayer only.

9

Single Life

Cross-cultural living and ministering make special demands upon single people because they lack the support and encouragement of a partner during the trying time of learning a language and adapting to the culture. They feel more acutely the loneliness and isolation of being a foreigner. Single missionaries should seek to have an open, meaningful relationship with one other person of the same sex. They need to be able to share on a significant level and pray about personal issues. This is vital for survival in a foreign culture away from the supportive structure of friends and family.

Advantages and disadvantages

Single people have some distinct advantages because they have more time for studying language, visiting and ministering among the people. They have more time for Bible study and prayer than their married colleagues who also have the care of children and spouse. The Apostle Paul commended the single life to Christians of his day in order that they may have *'undivided devotion to the Lord'* (see 1 Corinthians 7:32-35).

When considering some of the negative aspects of single life the above factors should be kept in mind to balance and keep issues in a proper perspective. Whatever our marital status, all of us need to view our true identity to be in Christ, rather than in human relationships. Marriage is a provision for this world only, as the Lord indicated in Matthew 22:30. Therefore, single people should live now with eternity in view. Then they can face hassles from that position, rather than being pressured by the world's standards.

I served thirteen years on the field as a single woman. The most common question I encountered was, 'Why aren't you married? Did you come here to find a husband?' The implication was that there had to be something wrong with anyone who was not married. Since the people could not understand the Christian view of marriage, I dismissed the subject by saying, 'God has not willed it', which satisfied my Muslim friends.

An unmarried woman is an oddity in many cultures. In the host country's society it may be that the only single women are widowed, divorced, or prostitutes. This makes it practically impossible for the people in some countries to accept single missionaries as normal people. When we visited in the village where I served, the children followed us around shouting '*sharamut*' (prostitute). This continued throughout the ten years we lived there.

The village people assumed that the married men on our mission compound visited all the women's homes at night in turn. That is how their men lived. Muslim men are allowed four wives and spend a night with each wife in rotation. Because the night watchman made the rounds of the hospital and homes throughout the night he was a help in correcting this false idea about our life style. As the activities of the foreigners was gossiped around the village, the night watchman broadcast the fact that the single women did not have men in their homes.

Single male missionaries are also viewed as oddities. Men who are not sexually active and thus have not produced children are thought of as boys, not men. That attitude makes it difficult for them to exercise a leadership role in such a society, even in the church. Some national people think it is their duty to provide the man with a woman and the women can be voluptuous and tempting. This sort of pressure is trying for a single man and demands a continual commitment of his sexuality to the Lord in order to live in such an environment.

Single missionaries battle with **loneliness**. This is more acute in early days on the field before meaningful relationships are established. However, it takes a different form in later years. The missionaries then may have become at home in the culture, with good friends among the ministry team and the nationals, but the time will come to retire. They may no longer have any real friends in the homeland. Also, if older, they may have the burden of aging parents and could well be called upon to go home to care for them.

Single women should not spend time with a man in a one-to-one situation such as discipling a man. He may show spiritual interest to allure her into a relationship and her loneliness could propel her into an unhealthy intimacy with the man. I know of several single women who have become emotionally involved this way which has led to problems and heartache. This caution is particularly relevant where the man is not a committed Christian.

Likewise, single women must control their relationships with male team members. This is especially important if there is a single male missionary on the team. He may seem to be very desirable to a single woman who might in other circumstances not give him a second thought. The isolation and the sparsity of available men there can distort her judgment. The culture in which they live and minister will also put restraints on male-female relationships. In many societies a friendly relationship between the sexes is unknown and any close relationship is assumed to be sexual. Therefore, it is important that single women avoid being alone with any man for a long period of time.

Another potential stumbling block for singles is the temptation to indulge in **self-pity**. Satan tempts us to long for what we do not have, keeping us from enjoying the legitimate friendships we do have. Singles may feel victimized, dwelling on the idea, 'If only I had a spouse and children of my own'. Any bitterness or self-pity which the missionary may harbor needs to be resolved. However hurtful their experiences may be, they need to learn lessons from it for personal growth and to handle similar situations in the future. If they were to look around, they would observe that many married people also suffer loneliness and frustrations. Single people can learn not to indulge in self-pity and be content in their appointed place in life. *'But godliness with contentment is great gain'* (1 Timothy 6:6).

Single missionaries may become possessive in their ministry. They may view the work and their converts to belong exclusively to them, since they have no family to call their own. They may think and speak of the work and converts in terms of 'my work' and 'my converts'. I know of one woman who would not pass over the names and addresses of her contacts for others to follow up while she was on home leave. All missionaries, whether single or married, need to keep in mind that we are involved in the Lord's work.

If single people live and work alone, they may become **inflexible**, intolerant and set in their ways. They should be encouraged to relate to others in the body of Christ so that wrong attitudes are challenged and the 'rough edges' of their character are smoothed. Singles can enjoy blessing and fulfillment in relating to missionary families on the ministry team. *'God sets the lonely in families'* (Psalm 68:6). Married missionaries may also be lonely, especially mothers of small children. Single and married can share in fellowship and prayer for mutual enrichment. Single people should respect a family's privacy, not visiting so often as to wear out their welcome. Also, families must not regard the single person as a free baby sitter.

Attitudes toward single women

Single women far outnumber single men on the mission field. Team leaders therefore need to acquire more understanding for the special needs of single women and show greater concern for them. Often they are devastated by the insensitive treatment received from within a mission agency. For example, they may be given no choice with whom they live, yet be expected to live harmoniously with someone they find incompatible. Married people at least have made a choice in the matter, for better or for worse.

A case illustrating the above issue is that of a first term missionary assigned to live and work with a senior woman. They were from different countries, their personalities clashed and they held opposite views on most topics. The senior missionary made no allowances for the new worker's lack of experience, calling her 'stupid' on many occasions. The new missionary endured the situation, trying to learn lessons from the Lord through it.

When she went to the area headquarters for medical attention, she shared her plight with the mission leader. She was told that there was no one to replace her at that locality and she would have to return there. As would be expected, she came home on furlough completely demoralized. She needed encouragement and assurance that she was loved and valued as a person.

That situation is an example of the need for team leaders to be sensitive to and care for single women with special needs.

I wish to make a comment without going into a theological discussion. In many Christian circles there is a stereotype role for single women. They are limited to exercising their gifts through serving food, teaching a Sunday school class and attending the prayer meeting. But the question must be asked, 'How do you reconcile the limitations on women's ministries in the home churches with their position on the mission field where they may carry full responsibility for the preaching, teaching and discipling?' We can hardly dismiss the question by saying there are not enough men to do the job. When we see the large number of men on the ministry teams in many of the home churches, we are compelled to conclude that the call to mission work for many men is, 'Here am I, Lord; send my sister!'

Mission agencies naturally reflect the attitudes of the Christian culture from which they originate. A large percentage of mission personnel is made up of single women. But generally they have little representation on the administrative, decision making level. Some men seem to feel threatened by competent women and are uncomfortable with women in an administrative role. Fortunately, this situation is being redressed in some mission agencies where the special gifts and insights of women are being utilized for the benefit of the group's ministry.

For further thought and action

1. You are single,
   a) What are some of your advantages in living in another culture?
   b) What potential problems might you face?

2. If you are married, how can you minister to fellow workers who are single?

3. What has been your attitude toward single women in ministry?
   Are there areas in which you need to change on this issue?

4. What strategy would you propose for mobilizing more men into missionary service?

10

Relating to Home Church and Supporters

My experience in serving on mission councils has impressed on me the direct link between missionaries' support and their correspondence with home churches. Those who faithfully keep their home churches informed about their ministry usually receive abundant prayer and financial support. Those who are not diligent in this matter are often poorly supported. Of course, we should look to the Lord to supply our needs, but he usually does it through people who share the common human weakness of 'out of sight, out of mind'. In other words, home congregations require reminders of their missionaries' needs.

Prayer letters

The demands upon missionaries' time and energy are great. Therefore, they must make a special effort to keep in touch with the people who support and pray for them. Writing letters may seem like a burden but it must be a high priority. Church members at home are also busy in their own lives and require regular reminding of the missionaries' needs.

Keeping a diary is a good practice. When a prayer letter is due you can look back at it and get ideas. Otherwise, in the busyness you forget what has been happening in past weeks or months. You should write to your prayer partners on a regular basis. It is helpful to have someone at home to print and mail the letters which are written to all on the mailing list. The following are some suggestions about prayer letters.

- Try to make letters interesting to readers, be creative and write on an informal, personal basis.
- Vary the content and format occasionally.
- Share human interest stories — about people witnessed to

and how some have trusted in Christ.
- Share answers to prayer and praise items.
- Have the children tell about their activities and prayer needs.
- Use some Scripture and spiritual messages but not a full sermon!
- Include photographs, 'one picture equals a thousand words'.
- Identify and define any foreign words used.
- Use initials for nationals' names for their protection, or if names are foreign to reader.
- Advise prayer partners about sensitive issues to be avoided in writing to you, e.g. references to political, religious, etc. conditions in your host country.
- Use a cassette occasionally, telling of work and prayer needs. Also, video cassettes if possible.
- Use electronic communication where possible for urgent messages.

Accountability

As a missionary, you are accountable to those who support you. You should not feel like a beggar but like a member of a team. You go and others provide the financial means. As the Apostle Paul wrote, '*Who at any time pays the expenses for doing military service? ... If we have sown spiritual good among you, is it too much if we reap your material benefits? If others share this rightful claim on you, do not we still more?*' (1 Corinthians 9:7,11,12, NRSV).

You must let supporters know that their gifts have been received and how the funds are being used. This gives them assurance that you are trustworthy and a good steward of funds. You should inform your supporters that their help is essential to the work and that they are a vital part of the ministry team.

Home leave

When you return to your homeland, you have special opportunities to relate to your home church, pastor and supporters. Rest and refreshment of body, soul and spirit are necessary, but home assignment is not one long vacation! It is simply a change in direction of ministry. You have a responsibility towards those who have supported you financially and by prayer. A good example is the Apostle Paul who returned to his home church in Antioch after one of his missionary journeys. *'On arriving there, they gathered the church together and reported all that God had done through them and how he had opened the door of faith to the Gentiles'* (Acts 14:27).

Home leave is a time for you to share in depth about the ministry in which you have been involved. You can share face to face matters about which it may be unwise to write in letters. Also, you can share your personal needs more honestly and help destroy the false concept that missionaries are 'super saints'. Avoid talking about 'my work' or 'my converts'. Present a wider vision of God's work in the world and yourself as a member of the team which Christ is using to build his church. *'So neither the one who plants nor the one who waters is anything, but only God who gives the growth'* (1 Corinthians 3:7, NRSV).

Well organized slides with commentary, a video of the work and overhead projector transparencies are useful in helping prayer partners see the people and the ministry among them. It will be necessary to prepare material while on the field. It is wise to take a variety of photographs and write down first impressions of the new culture early in your missionary life. You will find that the uniqueness of the people and environment become common place when you are busy and used to them.

You should share with church members in what ways the gospel has had an impact upon the people's lives; tell them stories of conversions, of the converts' own witness among their people, of the spiritual battles in that particular culture, of the maturing of the church. You should exalt the Lord Jesus when you speak of the work in which you have been involved and give him the glory for any accomplishment.

Re-entry stress

On a personal level, missionaries and their families face tremendous adjustments when they return to their homeland. You will probably expect a smooth re-entry but will experience culture shock in reverse. As stated previously, changes in our lives, good and bad, cause stress. Going back to your home country involves as many changes as going to the field because of the changes that will have taken place within the homeland in your absence. Also, you will have adapted your views and life-style to that of the host culture and will now feel like a stranger in your own country. In time missionaries become bicultural people, able to switch between home culture and host culture without too much stress and confusion.

Missionaries experience **mixed emotions** which others will not understand. You will enjoy being with family and friends again, being free of the constant demands of missionary work, and being enriched by the ministry of the home church. However, you will also feel sorrow over the loss of the strong bonds formed with people on the field. You will experience tiredness from all the travel and church meetings and disappointment over the moral decline in society. Also, you will be saddened by the worldliness in many churches, instead of concern for the world which they should have.

The responsibility of home churches and mission agencies to the missionary families on home leave will be covered in the next part of the book.

For further thought and action

1. What are your plans for keeping in touch with your prayer partners and supporters?

2. What suggestions from this chapter do you need to implement?

3. What is the scriptural basis for missionaries' financial support?

   How do you feel about being financially dependent?

4. What problems may you face when you return to your home country?

5. What preparations do you need to make now so you will have material to show your church about the work?

Part Two

Caring for Missionaries

Guidelines for Sending Churches and Mission Agencies

11

Selecting and Preparing Missionaries

This second part of the book offers suggestions for home churches and mission agencies in establishing procedures for assessment, selection, and preparation of missionary applicants. Also, the information is aimed at helping such groups to become more effective in caring for their missionaries, both on the field and at home.

Qualifications of applicants

The assessment of missionary applicants is a vital function of the sending churches and mission agencies. Co-operation between them is essential for the proper selection and preparation of missionaries. When assessing a couple, both husband and wife's suitability for cross-cultural living and working must be established. The husband's job/profession is not the only factor to be considered. The wife must be committed to missionary work herself and convinced her gifts will make a significant contribution to the ministry. I know of cases in which dissatisfied wives were the cause of early withdrawal of couples from the mission field.

Some of the qualifications of applicants which should be considered in assessing them are:

- Does the applicant have a strong relationship with the Lord which has been tested in hard times?
- Is the applicant seeking to live under the authority of the Scriptures?
- Does he/she demonstrate the qualities of character discussed in Chapter 2?
- Has he/she been active in sharing the gospel with others

and discipling them?
- What are the spiritual gifts of the applicant?
- How does the applicant relate to others: in church, at work, with friends and family?
- Has he/she been able to stick at a job, or has there been frequent moving and switching of jobs?
- Is the applicant emotionally stable so that he/she will not be moody or easily upset?
- Does the applicant have the mental stability needed in order to be relatively free from anxiety and depression?
- Can the pastor and mission committee confirm the applicant's call to missionary service?

All of these issues should be considered in assessing an applicant's suitability for missionary service. The answers to some of these questions will have to be obtained from experts.

Obtaining data for assessment

Perhaps the best predictor of applicants' suitability is their previous performance. They will tend to respond to new stresses and adjustments as they have handled life in the past. Therefore, it is necessary to collect data about applicants from several sources:

1. **An application form** filled out by the applicant. It should include biographical information, family and home life, educational and training data.

2. The applicant's **written testimony** of conversion and Christian growth, pattern of prayer and Bible study, Christian witness and service, leading toward missionary service.

3. **Referees' assessments** of the applicant from people nominated by applicant, including pastor and employer. The referees' form should encourage honest, objective answers about their character, Christian witness, relating to and working with others, attitude toward authority, competence in job or profession.

4. **Medical and psychological assessments** by specialists, with mission field conditions in mind. Is the applicant's health, mental and emotional stability, personal maturity adequate to enable them to cope with the stresses of cross-cultural living?

5. Written **doctrinal statement**, reviewed by a qualified per-

son. This should include the applicant's understanding of and commitment to the Christian doctrines held by the church and mission agency.

6. **Signed statement** by applicant of agreement to abide by the church and mission agency's policies and practices.

Preliminary interview

A few members of the church/mission committee should meet with the applicant. They should have in hand the information from the application form, Christian testimony, and referee's forms. During the interview, areas of personal life and sensitive matters can be explored, such as family background, any childhood trauma, sexual issues, marriage relationship, etc. This may reveal issues in the applicant's life which require counseling or the withdrawal of the application. The members should prayerfully make a decision about whether to proceed with the application and advise the applicant of their decision.

Final interview

When all the data from Numbers 1 — 6 above is available and the preliminary interview has been satisfactory, arrangements should be made for the final interview. The sending church may not have an organized missionary committee familiar with the requirements for missionary life and ministry. If not, they should appoint to the committee a capable person from a mission agency with such expertise. This person can give the committee guidance in the assessment and selection of applicants.

Some members may be unskilled in interviewing and there may be new members on the committees. Therefore, a form to assist interviewing would be helpful. A structured procedure facilitates the best use of time and ensures that all important areas are considered in the interview. It will also enable all members of the interview panel to participate. Also, not all members will be familiar with missionary life, so it will be beneficial to review 'Special Stresses of Missionary Life' in Chapter 2.

Before the interview the chairperson should make sure that all committee members are familiar with the information gained from the data collected by the above means. This will help the committee learn which areas need exploring during interview. The questions listed at the beginning of this chapter concerning the qualifications of applicants should be kept in mind during the interview.

The chairperson should invite the applicant into the meeting and introduce them to all committee members. The applicant should be made to feel at ease and encouraged to share freely without any fear of judgment or criticism. The chairperson then states the purpose of the interview: to discern the applicant's suitability for living and ministering in another culture.

Use of Questions

The interview will be enhanced if the applicant verbalizes points about their conversion, Christian life, relationships, attitudes, etc., even though the committee has the written data. Questions should be stated in such a way as to gain the most information. For example, the questions should require thoughtful self-awareness and self-revelation on the part of the applicant in order to answer properly. Questions which can be answered by a simple 'yes' or 'no' should be avoided because this does not adequately reveal how the applicant is thinking. Phrase questions by asking,

'How do you feel about ...?'
'What do you think about ...?'
'What do you think would happen if ...?'
'Would you share with us ...?'
'How would you explain to someone that ...?'

Just as phrasing the questions correctly is the committee's responsibility, so is the interpretation of the applicant's answers. Few applicants would deliberately seek to deceive the committee, but someone may have an unconscious desire to please and be accepted which motivates them to try to say the right thing. There is therefore an obligation on committee members to listen carefully to the applicant's answers and to detect genuine motivation and responses.

From the answers to the questions, and the way the applicant answers, the committee members should be able to determine the applicant's ability to communicate, to express ideas and to solve theoretical problems. Also, the applicant's likely attitude and reaction in certain situations will become evident. The committee should gain sufficient information from the interview to make a recommendation about the applicant's service with the church/mission agency.

In drawing the interview to a close, the chairperson should invite the applicant to express any doubts or questions they may have. Questions the committee cannot answer must be referred to a person who can give the applicant the information they seek. The committee members then should commit the applicant to the Lord in prayer. The applicant should be assured that they will be informed about the outcome of the interview and the next step to be taken.

Further training

The committee may advise the applicant to take a Bible College course, depending on their biblical and theological knowledge. More experience in evangelism, discipling and church planting may also be desirable. Also, missionary training in subjects such as cultural anthropology, cross-cultural communication, cultural adaptation, linguistics, making the gospel relevant in a culture, and study of the religion of the target people group is also advisable.

The sending church should make a sacrificial commitment to the proper preparation of their missionary applicant. This may involve sponsorship for training in a regional center where the above subjects are taught. Remember, the missionary is the church's representative to another people group. They cannot share the gospel effectively if inadequately prepared.

Sending churches should understand the need for and the potential ministry of 'tent makers'. These are Christians who live and work cross-culturally by virtue of their job/profession. This may be the only means of Christian witness in countries where ordinary missionary work is prohibited. The prayers and encouragement of their home church are essential for their survival and effectiveness, even though they may not need financial support. The old idea that only those who preach are real missionaries is no longer valid in today's world. Christians who work overseas in a secular job or relief work and have a concern for the spiritual welfare of the people around them, are ambassadors for Christ. Home churches can help prepare them for the spiritual ministry and warfare in which they will be involved.

Commissioning service and departure

When the missionaries are prepared to go to the field and the church has made its commitment to pray, support and encourage them, then a special commissioning service should be held. This should be a joint effort by the church and mission agency. It involves a message of encouragement for the missionaries and family, the laying on of hands by the elders and prayer for the missionaries' service. It ought to be a significant time for the missionaries and the congregation alike, a reminder of their commitment before the Lord and to one another.

There are many practical issues in which the church can assist the missionary family regarding departure for another country. In the final days they may need help with housing, meals, use of a car, financial assistance after quitting a job, the shipment of freight to the field, arrangements for travel to the field, and travel to the airport for departure. Such matters need to be discussed with the missionaries and also with their extended families who will be involved in the plans.

It would be a great encouragement to the missionary to have some of the members of the church and mission agency see them off at the airport. Also, it helps the extended family at home to know the missionaries are well cared for. One of the members should commit the missionaries and their travel to the Lord. It may be appropriate to sing together a chorus or hymn. All such demonstrations of loving care give the missionaries great encouragement and precious memories. This is important to them as they leave all they love and know for the sake of Christ and the extension of his kingdom.

For further thought and action

Review the Case Study of letters from a missionary applicant in Chapter 1. Think about how your church would handle an applicant like Paul. Are the pastor and church committed to missions as a high priority? Or, is it just an optional extra for which a few members are concerned? Is the church organized to help in the selection and preparation of mission applicants? These issues and the following questions should be seriously considered by the pastor and congregation.

1. Are you praying now for the Lord to raise up missionaries from your own congregation?

2. Are the members accepting their responsibility to fulfill the 'Great Commission' (Matthew 28:19,20) by praying and giving to missions?

3. Do you have a functioning Missions Committee? If not, what action needs to be taken?

4. Is there a strong prayer group who will uphold missionaries sent out by the church?

5. Does the church budget allow for financial support of missionaries? If not, what changes need to be made?

6. Would the church be prepared to help missionaries financially with further training?

7. Is the church in contact with a mission agency through which you can channel missionary applicants? If not, how do you plan to send and support them on the field?

12

Caring for Missionaries on the Field

Role of home churches and mission agencies

Home churches and pastors should play a supportive role in a missionary's ministry, not a controlling one. There needs to be a chain of command for the missionary on the field which is understood and honored by all concerned. The missionary is accountable to the home supportive group but decisions concerning the work on the field need to be made by team members in that country. Many factors which affect the work are constantly changing. It requires someone familiar with the situation and culture to deal with the changes.

There are definite advantages to missionaries working within an established mission agency. The issues were stated in Chapter 2 and are worth repeating here. The mission agencies are able to set up structures for language learning and orientation to the particular ministry of each missionary. Also, mission agencies develop experience in dealing with national governments, obtaining visas and work permits, arranging transport within the country and purchasing supplies for missionaries in isolated areas. They provide medical and dental care for their personnel and schooling for the children.

There should be no sense of rivalry between sending church and mission agency. Each has a role to fulfill in obeying Christ's mandate, roles which are complementary not competitive. The church is the sending and supportive body. The mission agency is the channel, with special expertise, which enables the missionaries to live and minister in a foreign culture. The following is a case showing the importance of this issue:

A couple were sent out as missionaries by their local church. They were assessed and accepted by a large mission group working in the country to which they felt called. The mission recommended Bible college training and arranged for the couple to go to Australia for training. When the couple completed their training, the mission contacted the field and asked for a letter from the national church to invite the new missionaries to work there. This is a necessary procedure in many countries where the church work is nationalized. Governments demand such a letter in order to grant an entry visa for nationals from other countries.

The couple wrote to their pastor telling him they were waiting for the visa. He wrote back, ordering them to proceed to the field without delay. To him it seemed they were just wasting time in Australia where they had trained. He felt they should move on to their missionary work. The couple believed they should follow the pastor's orders since their pastor and home church were supporting them. They left Australia against the mission group's advice. Landing on the field without entry visas and without approval of the national church, the confusion and problems for all concerned are all too apparent.

Another issue which the sending churches must face is the pressure they put upon their missionaries for 'success stories'. I know missionaries who had support dropped by their churches because there had been no spectacular results within a certain period of time. We must keep in mind the words of commendation by the Lord Jesus, '*Well done good and* **faithful** *servant*' (Matthew 25:23). He does not say, '*successful* servant', nor does he measure success by the world's standards.

Sending out Pastors and Specialists

If the home church and pastor want a more active role in their missionary's ministry, they can send the pastor or mission committee members to visit the field. In that way they gain deeper insight into the missionaries' work, their needs and the problems of establishing the church in that culture. When the visitors return home, they can share their insights with the congregation. Then, all will be better equipped to pray for and support the missionaries on the field.

Qualified people are always welcome on the field to conduct seminars for missionaries on relevant subjects, such as, communication, conflict resolution, counseling, management skills, etc.

Also, pastors can be involved through spiritual life conferences in which weary missionaries are spiritually renewed and encouraged. Churches and mission agencies need to combine resources to send teams to the field for this type of ministry.

Medical teams can make a significant contribution in areas where the needs are great and the health care is limited. For example, we had an eye specialist visit our hospital when I was on the field. The specialist and his trained nurse arrived with the special instruments required. Their work was done on a voluntary basis without any compensation, other than the joy of restoring people's sight.

Other specialists able to make useful visits to the field in developing countries are builders, plumbers, electricians, motor mechanics and agriculturalists. Such services are desperately needed on many mission fields.

Pastoral care on the field

Care of missionaries in areas of their personal life is an important aspect of mission work. This is especially vital to their welfare in their early days on the field. They need to have senior workers assigned to them personally to act as 'shepherds' through the early adjustment period. Senior missionaries can advise new members in cultural and language learning and can counsel and encourage the new people as they battle with the stresses of early field adjustments. Senior missionaries also serve as role models for the new. Therefore, it is important for senior persons to demonstrate godly attitudes and relationships with fellow workers, nationals and church leaders. Home church members and pastors can through letters encourage their missionaries to heed the senior shepherd's advice and to develop a proper attitude toward authority on the field.

Missionaries also need pastoral care and counseling. Fellow workers may be too busy to give in-depth counseling. Each field should have a person designated to provide this care, someone qualified in counseling who understands the pressures of missionary life. Home churches may be instrumental in supplying such a person. A group of churches, along with a mission agency, can cooperate in selecting and financing a pastor or counselor to make a prolonged visit to the field. The person needs to make a commitment of several months to the job as it takes time to win missionaries' trust. More details about counseling missionaries will be covered in the following chapter.

The sending church members, through personal letters and cards on special occasions such as birthdays, can provide a ministry of encouragement to their missionaries. This personal concern for them means a great deal to missionaries who often feel lonely and isolated. Cassette recordings of church services, sermons and expositions of books of the Bible are a real boost to tired missionaries who may struggle to have meaningful Bible studies by themselves. When I was on the field, we welcomed good spiritual teaching on cassettes for our own worship services. In some Muslim areas there are no churches where expatriates can worship and fellowship. Our only church service was held in our homes and members of the team took turns bringing the message. We were all blessed when a guest preacher, via tape recording, gave us edifying Bible teaching.

For further thought and action

1. If your missionaries were in a situation similar to that of the couple in the case story of this chapter, what advice would you give them?

2. Does your church have links with a reputable mission agency on the field with which you can associate and link your missionaries?

3. What action should be taken to have regular updates on your missionaries in your church services?

4. Consider how your congregation can be involved in pastoral care of your missionaries on the field.

5. What steps need to be taken by the church members to participate in writing to and encouraging your missionaries?

6. Are there professional people or tradesmen in your congregation who could visit the field and use their skills to help the over worked, under staffed missionaries?

13

Caring for Missionaries in the Homeland

Provision for material needs

What are the responsibilities of the sending church and mission agency toward their missionaries when they return home? It would be good to now review the issues discussed in Chapter 10 to get a better understanding of how missionaries struggle with their adjustments. Preparations for their return home should be made well in advance. Co-operation between the mission agencies and home churches is essential. Both groups must work for the welfare of the missionaries, not for the advancement of their group. Of course, missionaries will be making their own plans but there needs to be coordination of all programs. Also, missionaries' relatives need to be considered in all arrangements.

Some issues that need to be thought through and addressed by all concerned are:

- Who will meet the missionaries' plane?
- Where will they sleep and eat upon arrival?
- What about an early holiday and rest?
- Where will they set up home base? How will housing, furnishings, etc. be provided?
- Who will provide transport for their home leave?
- How will their financial support be provided?
- What about scheduling meetings with home churches?
- Where will the children attend school and will extra funds be needed?
- What further training will they need for future ministry?

An excellent resource for home churches and mission agencies in dealing with these issues is the book, *Love your Local Missionary*. In the chapter, 'The Missionary at Home', Dr Anne

Townsend offers many suggestions of practical ways church groups can help missionaries adjust. She points out the necessity of being sensitive to their personal needs.

'However, make sure that your missionary has the time and space for the kind of spiritual renewal and fresh encounter with God that he needs. He may be wounded and tired from the battle; he may be discouraged; he may want to give up; the sacrifice he faces on return may seem more than he can render; or he may quite simply be exhausted in every fibre of his being. Give him the opportunity for renewal.' [1]

I shared with a couple who had profound problems in their family life, as well as in ministry on the field. The issues they faced could not be resolved by a few sessions with a counselor, though that was a start. Fortunately, the Lord met their needs through the warm, supportive fellowship of their local church. They found the loving acceptance and personal encouragement needed to work out their personal issues. As I listened to them tell what this fellowship within the body of Christ meant to them, my heart cried, 'O, Lord, raise up more churches like this who will care for missionaries that have been honorably wounded!'

Pastoral care

Dr Townsend also has a word to pastors:

'Never feel that your missionary is so spiritual and so perfect that he doesn't need the ordinary kind of pastoring that other sheep in God's flock need. If you think that way, you delude yourself! Your missionary has spiritual needs, deficiencies and strengths in the same way that each member of the body of Christ has them![2]

In view of all the stresses missionaries face, it is obvious that they require special care, both on the field and at home. Sending churches and mission agencies should be aware of their need. The purpose of pastoral caring and counseling for missionaries is to encourage them and to facilitate their growth through the difficulties they experience. *'Let us consider how we may spur one another on toward love and good deeds ... let us encourage*

---

[1] Edited by Martin Goldsmith. England: STL and MARC, 1984, p. 49.
[2] p. 51

one another...' (Hebrews 10:24,25). My book *Encouragement and Growth for Every Missionary* addresses this need (see the Suggested Reading list).

Missionaries are very human like the rest of us, subject to personal failings. The assumption that full time Christian service somehow releases people from their struggles with old patterns of thinking and behaving is wrong. On the contrary, these areas of personal battles are intensified by the stresses of their work and the opposition of Satan. Also, they are just as prone to pride and deceitfulness of heart as others are. They need members of the body of Christ to admonish them and godly counseling to help them admit their failings. The only way to forgiveness and restoration of fellowship with the Lord and others is through confession of sinfulness. '*...let us throw off everything that hinders and the sin that so easily entangles, and let us run with perseverance the race marked out for us. Let us fix our eyes on Jesus, the author and perfecter of our faith*' (Hebrews 12:1,2).

Objectives in pastoral care and counseling of missionaries are:

- to help them use their experiences for learning lessons and maturing in Christ.
- to affirm and encourage those who appear to be coping well.
- to help missionaries resolve inner conflicts so that they may be more effective in their Christian life and ministry.
- to lovingly confront those who are demonstrating wrong attitudes and behavior, and to help them change.
- to strengthen relationships with fellow workers, nationals, and mission/team leaders for the future.
- to facilitate restoration of the wounded to wholeness of body, soul, and spirit.
- to enable those on home leave to have a joyful, meaningful time, strengthening links with churches and supporters.
- to prepare them for return to the field with a positive outlook.

Counseling and debriefing program

The following is a description of a debriefing and counseling program which can serve as a model for groups who are establishing this type of care for their members. This material was first published in my book, *Personal Encouragement and Growth for Every Missionary*. For ten years, I conducted a debriefing and counseling program for all missionaries on home assignment in SIM Australia. It was expanded to include ten mission agencies. A total of ninety-two missionaries participated in the program. Anyone who has experienced the stresses of missionary life will probably have some unresolved issues. Therefore, I tailored the program for all members, not just those who needed counseling for specific problems. Most mission groups require their personnel on home leave to have a medical examination and treatment. In the same way, an assessment and care of their mental/emotional status should be available for all.

The debriefing by mission agencies usually pertains to the work and does not cover personal issues. Every missionary has probably experienced some hurts, disappointments, and conflicts which need to be explored and resolved. Debriefing of couples must deal equally with the husband and wife's experiences and struggles. Many missionaries carry their internal stresses from the field to their homeland and back to the field, simply because no one takes time to share and care. I suffered this way myself during missionary service and have become aware through counseling that many others do too.

The basis of the counseling program was directive, biblical counseling which applied scriptural principles to various aspects of life and ministry. The aim of the counseling was to provide personal encouragement and promote maturing in Christ for all missionaries as they dealt with different experiences and problems in their lives. It should be emphasized that the program included all missionaries. This prevented any one feeling that they were being singled out as a 'problem person'. It also corrected the idea that counseling is only for those suffering a breakdown.

A questionnaire which covers all the major areas of missionary life was formulated, the **Personal Evaluation of Field Experience (P.E.F.E.)**. A copy was sent with an explanatory letter, asking the missionary to mark it prayerfully and honestly. The form was to be marked in each area on a scale of 1 to 10 according to how they coped. Then the missionary arranged a session with the counselor. The questionnaire served as a spring-board for the counseling session since it highlighted the issues with which the missionary was struggling. A sample of the P.E.F.E. form follows (see next page). It may be copied and used by groups wishing to implement debriefing and counseling for their members.

Counselors should send a report of general observations about the missionary's psychological and emotional status to the church/mission director. Also, recommendations for follow-up care as indicated are noted. This is necessary for the planning of the missionary's rest period, meetings with churches, and eventual return to the field.

Counselors can be drawn from the ranks of pastors, psychologists, and trained counselors, preferably with some under-standing of missionary life. Retired people from these groups can be a great asset to missions since they have a lifetime of experience and are relatively free from other commitments. Such people may be in short supply in emerging mission areas. Churches and mission agencies need to combine with other groups in order to find the resources for a counseling program, i.e. finances and qualified personnel, etc. A regional center can be established to which missionaries are referred.

Counselors should be allowed to exercise their role within the doctrinal and ethical boundaries acceptable to the church/mission agency. The counselors' job description and accountability must be clearly defined. Also, procedures should be formulated for regular review of the effectiveness of the counselors and the program.

(CONFIDENTIAL)   (P.E.F.E. Form)

Personal Evaluation of Field Experience

Note: To facilitate marking, a simple gradation system of 1-10 is used; 1 = poor, 10 = good. Assess yourself under each topic according to your average, prevailing condition/coping in that area. Use blank spaces or back page to add statements which clarify your marks.

1. PERSONAL AREAS of LIFE

Physical: 1 (poor) — 10 (good)

General health :
     Regular exercise   . . . .
     Amount of rest   . . . .
     Balanced diet   . . . .
     Sleeping pattern   . . . .

Preventive measures:
     Malaria tabs.   . . . .
     Booster shots   . . . .
     Sanitary conditions   . . . .
     Holiday breaks   . . . .

Spiritual: 1 (poor) — 10 (good)
     Consistent devotions   . . . .
     Witnessing to others   . . . .
     Regular Bible study   . . . .
     Fellowship with others . . . .
     Prayer life   . . . .

Mental: 1 (seldom) — 10 (often)
     Reading in profession/job . . . .
     Reading in world affairs . . . .
     Reading good literature . . . .
     Pursuing hobbies   . . . .

Emotional: 1 (seldom) — 10 (often)

     Sense of joy   . . . .

     Sense of contentment   . . . .

     Sense of self-worth   . . . .

     Optimism   . . . .

     Loneliness   . . . .

     Anxiety, fear   . . . .

     Depression   . . . .

     Resentment, unforgiveness   . . . .

2. MARRIAGE and FAMILY LIFE:

                    1 (conflict) — 10 (harmony)

Communication with spouse: . . . .

Unity :

     Sexual relations   . . . .

     Soul (personalities)   . . . .

     Spiritual   . . . .

Parenting:

     Care of children   . . . .

     Discipline of children   . . . .

     Education of children   . . . .

Time with family vs. work:

     Wife/Mother   . . . .

     Husband/Father   . . . .

3. SINGLENESS ISSUES:

Living with others: 1 (difficult) — 10 (easy)

     Running household   . . . .

     Adjusting to habits   . . . .

Handling:

     Need for affection   . . . .

     Singleness and sexual tensions . . . .

     Attitudes of

     others toward singles   . . . .

Handling of low status of women:

     Within Team Mission   . . . .

     Among nationals   . . . .

4. INTER-PERSONAL RELATIONSHIPS:

1 (difficult) — 10 (easy)

Adjusting to fellow workers . . . .
Close friendships with colleagues . . . .
Resolving conflicts with colleagues . . . .
Forgiving offenses of others . . . .
Close friendships with nationals . . . .
Resolving conflicts with nationals . . . .

5. CROSS-CULTURAL ADJUSTMENTS:

1 (poor) — 10 (good)

Language Aptitude:

Available language learning aids . . . .
Persistence in learning . . . .
Ability to hear language . . . .
Ability to verbalize . . . .
Communication of gospel . . . .

Cultural Adaptation:

Mission group's field orientation . . . .
Acceptance of cultural differences . . . .
Coping with own foreignness . . . .
Handling own racism . . . .
Rapport with national people . . . .

Relating to National Church:

Fellowship with national Christians . . . .
Your ministry within national church . . . .
Working with/under national leaders . . . .

6. MINISTRY/ JOB:

1 (little) — 10 (much)

Similarity of anticipated job and actual job . . . .
Sense of job/ministry satisfaction . . . .
Desire to continue same job/ministry . . . .
Success in maintaining priorities . . . .
Difficulty in managing time . . . .
Cooperation from others . . . .
Encouragement from others . . . .

7. MISSION/TEAM LEADERSHIP:

                                          1 (poor) — 10 (good)

Supervision of missionaries   . . . .
Communication with missionaries   . . . .
Your evaluation of field leadership   . . . .
Your agreement with policies and strategy . . . .
Care of missionaries' personal needs   . . . .
Education for children   . . . .

SUMMARY:

In general terms, would you say your experience has been:

                                                   (yes/no)

Satisfying   . . . .
Disillusioning   . . . .
Had the effect of maturing you   . . . .
Would prompt you to
recommend similar service to others   . . . .

(NOTE: This form is CONFIDENTIAL and is to be viewed only by the counselor.)

Major Areas of Stress Revealed in Program

The major areas of tension which missionaries revealed during counseling are listed below. 'Significant struggles' indicate the percentage of missionaries who marked each area. The item on the P.E.F.E. form was considered 'significant' if marked 4 or less, on the scale of 1-10. (1 = poor/difficult; 10 = good/easy)

1. PERSONAL AREAS   Significant Struggles

Spiritual Areas:
a. Prayer and devotional life .34%
b. Bible study 34%
c. Witnessing for Christ 44%

Mental and Emotional:
a. Loneliness 17%
b. Fear 23%
c. Low self-image 29%
d. Depression 37%
e. Resentment 40%

2. MARRIAGE and FAMILY:
a. Parenting 21%
b. Communicating with partner 37%
c. Relational disharmony: body, soul, spirit 50%

3. SINGLE LIFE:
a. Need of affection 33%
b. Low status of women 55%
c. No choice of house mate .66%

4. INTER-PERSONAL RELATIONSHIPS:
a. Lack of close friendships .26%
b. Adjusting to other expatriates 43%
c. Resolving conflicts: with expats. 49%
                          with nat'ls 23%

5. CROSS-CULTURAL ADJUSTMENTS:
a. Foreignness 14%
b. Language learning 31%
c. Inadequate field orientation 34%

6. MINISTRY/JOB:
a. Unfulfilled in job 26%
b. Unreal expectations 26%
c. Working under inefficiency 29%
d. Maintaining priorities 31%
e. Lack of cooperation and encouragement 31%

7. TENSIONS in MISSION/TEAM:
a. Area leadership and strategy 43%
b. Communication with leadership 46%
c. Supervision of new missionaries 57%

8. SUMMARY of FIELD EXPERIENCE:
a. Found it maturing process 86%
b. Would recruit others to go   NO 9%
                                 YES 91%

Conclusions and recommendations:

Some significant conclusions were drawn, based on the findings of the counseling program for normally functioning missionaries. The need for a counseling program encompassing all stages of missionaries' career was noted.

1. Missionaries are subject to extremely stressful situations, and require special care of the whole person, body, soul, spirit.

2. Counseling is an essential aspect of that care, especially regarding missionaries' emotional and psychological welfare.

3. Counseling is effective in helping missionaries mature in Christ.

4. Most missionaries are open to counseling and find it helpful.

5. Missionaries would benefit from effective counseling on the field.

6. Specific problem areas for those counseled were identified:

a) Several major problems in personal life and in marriages were found to have been present before field experience.

b) Single women have unique needs, often ignored by insensitive team leaders.

c) Cross-cultural stress was often aggravated by lack of support and direction from senior missionaries.

d) Inter-personal conflict causes personal stress; Satan uses it to sow dissension among workers.

e) Some Mission/Team leaders were found to be inadequate in communication and supervision of members.

7. The attrition rate of missionaries could be reduced with relevant counseling at all stages of their lives.[3]

- Stage 1   Applicants: Preparatory and Preventive Counseling
- Stage 2   First Term: Encouragement and Growth Counseling
- Stage 3   Senior Missionaries and Mission Leaders: Personal Maturing, Counseling others
- Stage 4   Retired/Repatriated Missionaries: Redeployment Counseling

---

[3] Details of counseling missionaries throughout their careers can be found in the article: 'Let My People Grow', by Dr J.A. Dennett, *Evangelical Missions Quarterly*, April, 1990, pp. 147-152. Also, in my book found in the Suggested Reading list.

For further thought and action

1. What plans need to be made for your returning missionaries in regard to the questions at the beginning of this chapter?

2. How can your church and mission agency cooperate to provide pastoral care and counseling for your missionaries?

3. Do you have any trained counselors in your church, or contact with any, who can help solve No. 2 above?

4. Consider organizing a regional center which can provide counseling and debriefing of missionaries.

5. The Missions Committee should study the 'Major areas of Stress' listed. Then, consider how you might help alleviate some of those stresses for your missionaries.

6. What books about missions are in your church library?

7. What books and articles should your church obtain and study in order to be more effective in missionary endeavor? Review the 'Suggested Reading' list at the end of this book.

Suggested Reading

Anderson, J. N. (1984) *Christianity and World Religions.* Downers Grove, IL:Inter-Varsity Press.

Brewster, E.T. & E.S. (1976) *Language Acquisition Made Practical (LAMP): Field Methods for Language Learners.* Colorado Springs, CO: Lunga House.

Dennett, W. D. (1996) *Sharing God's Love with Muslims: Effective Guidelines for Christians.* South Holland, IL: The Bible League.

Evangelical Missions Quarterly, Published by the E.M.I.S., P O Box 794, Wheaton, IL 60189.

Fuller, Lois (1991) *The Missionary and His Work.* Jos, Nigeria: Capro Media Services, PO Box 6001, Jos, Nigeria.

Hesselgrave, D.J. (1984) *Communicating Christ Cross-culturally.* Grand Rapids, MI: Zondervan.

Johnstone, P. (1993) *Operation World.* Wayneboro, GA: STL.

Larson, D.N. (1984) *Guidelines for Barefoot Language Learning.* St. Paul, MN: CMS.

Lewis, J. (editor) (1993) *Working your Way to the Nations: A Guide to Effective Tentmaking.* Pasadena, CA: William Carey Library.

Lingenfelter, S.G. & Mayers, M.K.(1986) *Ministering Cross-culturally.* Grand Rapids, MI: Baker Book House.

Loss, Myron (1983) *Culture Shock: Dealing with Stress in Cross-cultural Living.* Winona Lake, IN: Light & Life Press.

Pate, Larry (1989) *From Every People: A Handbook of Two-thirds World Missions with Directory/Histories/Analysis.* MARC/OC Ministries. Available from OC Ministries, 25 Corning Ave., Milpitas, CA 95035-5336.

Taylor, William David (editor) (1991) *Internationalizing Missionary Training: A Global Perspective.* Grand Rapids, MI: Baker Book House.

Winter, R. & Hawthorne, S.C. (editors) (1992) *Perspectives on the World Christian Movement: A Reader*. Pasadena, CA: William Carey Library.

Yamamori, T. (1993) *Penetrating Missions' Final Frontier: A New Strategy for Unreached Peoples*. Downers Grove, IL: Inter-Varsity Press.

Care of Missionaries:

Dennett, J.A. (1990) *Personal Encouragement and Growth for Every Missionary*. Australia: Gospel & Missionary Society. (Distributed by SIM International home offices.)

Foyle, Marjory (1987) *Honourably Wounded: Stress among Christian Workers*. England: MARC.

Goldsmith, Martin (editor) (1984) *Love your Local Missionary*. England: STL & MARC.

O'Donnell, K.S. & M.L. (1988) *Helping Missionaries Grow: Readings in Mental Health and Missions*. Pasadena, CA: William Carey Library.